Securing a Level 4
Mathematics
Teacher's Book

Hilary Koll and Steve Mills

D1148244

RISING STARS

Rising Stars UK Ltd.
22 Grafton Street, London W1S 4EX
www.risingstars-uk.com

Every effort has been made to trace copyright holders and obtain their permission for the use of copyright materials. The authors and publisher will gladly receive information enabling them to rectify any error or omission in subsequent editions.

All facts are correct at time of going to press.

Published 2010

Authors: Hilary Koll and Steve Mills
Consultant Maths Publisher: Jean Carnall
Text design: Laura de Grasse
Typesetting: Ray Rich
Artwork: David Woodroffe
Cover Design: Burville-Riley Partnership

British Library Cataloguing in Publication Data.
A CIP record for this book is available from the British Library.

ISBN: 978-1-84680-720-6

Printed by Ashford Colour Press

Contents

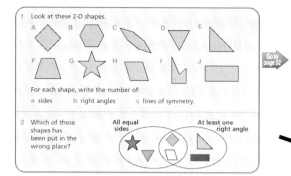

Unit 6 – System scan A

1. Look at these 2-D shapes.

   A B C D E

   F G H I J

   For each shape, write the number of:
   a sides   b right angles   c lines of symmetry.

   Go to page 52

2. Which of these shapes has been put in the wrong place?

   All equal sides   At least one right angle

3. Answer these questions.
   a What shapes are the faces of a cube?
   b How many faces does a triangular prism have?
   c How many vertices does a square-based pyramid have?
   d How many vertices does a cuboid have?
   e What is special about the edges of a cube?
   f How many edges does a cylinder have?

   Go to page 54

4. Decide whether these statements are **true** or **false**.
   a BG is parallel to AF.
   b CD is perpendicular to DH.
   c AE is parallel to DH.
   d EC is perpendicular to CI.

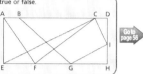

   Go to page 56

10

1

Review and Assess

Written and mental questions help teachers identify what pupils know, where there are gaps in their knowledge and to highlight misconceptions.

5

Review and Assess

Review learning and ask the pupils to complete the Check-up scan. This helps them check they're confident with all aspects of the key objectives covered.

Check-up scan 6C   Name: _____

1 Tick to show whether each statement is **true** or **false**.

   True? False?

   a BG is parallel to AF.
   b AF is perpendicular to FC.
   c FE is parallel to CD.
   d GI is perpendicular to CI.
   e AE is parallel to HI.
   f FC is perpendicular to CI.

2 Colour the true statements.

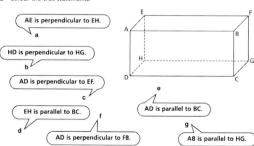

   a AE is perpendicular to EH.
   b HD is perpendicular to HG.
   c AD is perpendicular to EF.
   d EH is parallel to BC.
   e AD is parallel to BC.
   f AD is perpendicular to FB.
   g AB is parallel to HG.

Train your brain!

Draw a pentagon that has both parallel sides and perpendicular sides, on the back of this sheet.

I can name shapes and describe their properties, using mathematical language.
I can recognise parallel and perpendicular sides.

74   © Rising Stars Ltd. 2010   Shine!/Level 4 Check-up scan 6C

pproach
a level

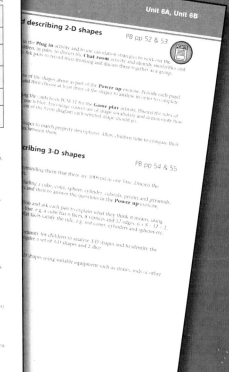

2

each

e the clear teachers notes
help you address the gaps
ing a range of activities
cluding mental maths
uestions, opportunities to
lk about mathematics
d hands-on
tivities.

Practise

3

Practice questions, games
and activities give pupils
lots of opportunities to
gain confidence in key areas.

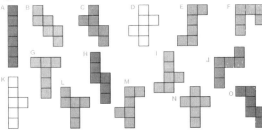

Apply

nce pupils are
ecure in their
nowledge and
nderstanding, the
xplore questions
nable them to utilise
heir skills in different
ontexts and to solve
mathematical
roblems.

4

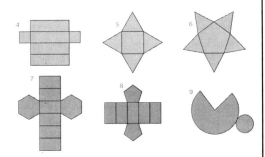

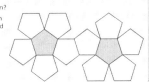

Unit 1 Securing mental skills

The mental skills outlined below are integral to other areas of mathematics and, thus, are addressed throughout the book. The table below details in which units of the book each objective is predominantly addressed, although many aspects occur in virtually all units, e.g. building up speed with mental calculation.

To focus on mental skills, pupils can first complete the 'System scan' pages for Unit 1 (pages 4 and 5). Observe the specific areas of difficulty, referring to the 'Errors and misconceptions' list of notes below for further information. Areas of weakness then can be addressed through some or all of the units suggested. Finally, the related 'Check-up scan' sheet or sheets can be given as an assessment, focusing particularly on the questions detailed in the final column below.

Securing mental skills objectives	Included in Units	Follow-up assessments
• understand and use language associated with the four operations, for example, difference, sum, total, product, multiple, share equally, factor, remainder	2F, 5B, 6E	Check-up scan 2F q1 Check-up scan 5B q1 Check-up scan 6E q1
• build on what they know, for example, $624 \div 6 = (600 \div 6) + (24 \div 6) = 100 + 4 = 104$	2D, 2F, 3D, 4D, 6D	Check-up scan 2D q3 Check-up scan 6D q1
• recognise cases where particular strategies will be effective, for example, using rounding to work out that £1.99 × 3 = £6.00 − 3p	2C, 3D, 3E	Check-up scan 2C q4 Check-up scan 3D q1 Check-up scan 3E q4
• answer simple decimal calculations, using their relationship to number facts, for example, $0.7 \times 3 = 2.1$ as 7 tenths × 3 = 21 tenths or 2.1; $5.4 \div 9 = 0.6$ as $9 \times 6 = 54$ and $9 \times 0.6 = 5.4$	2C, 2D, 2E, 2F, 3D, 4C	Check-up scan 2C q3 Check-up scan 2D q3 Check-up scan 2E q2 Check-up scan 2F q1 and q2 Check-up scan 3D q1 and q2 Check-up scan 4C q2
• use number lines and other notes to record working clearly	2F, 3B, 3C, 5E	Check-up scan 3B q2 and q3 Check-up scan 3C q3 Check-up scan 5E q1 and q2
• build up speed with practice for calculations that can be done mentally	2D, 2F, 3B, 3D, 4C, 4D, 5A, 5B, 5D, 5E, 6D	Check-up scan 2D q2 Check-up scan 3B q3 Check-up scan 3D q1 Check-up scan 4C q1 Check-up scan 4D q1 Check-up scan 5B q1 Check-up scan 5D q1 Check-up scan 5E q1 and q2 Check-up scan 6D q1
• answer questions involving units mentally, for example, find the number of millilitres in $\frac{1}{5}$ of a litre	2C, 2F, 3D, 4C, 6B, 6D	Check-up scan 2C q4 Check-up scan 3D q1 Check-up scan 4C q1 Check-up scan 6B q1 Check-up scan 6D q1

Key vocabulary

digit, place value, number, numeral, position, units/ones, tens, hundreds, thousands, tens of thousands, hundreds of thousands, millions, number lines, multiple, factor, difference, product, sum, total, share, remainder, round, estimate, mental method, notes, calculator, decimal, strategy, multiply, divide, share, times, groups of, lots of, equal groups, counting on, counting back, number sentence, recall, chunking, array

Notes on securing mental methods through oral and starter activities

- Ensure that children regularly rehearse addition and subtraction facts and multiplication and division facts in oral activities. Encourage them to relate these facts to a wide range of contexts and situations, and also to use them to find new and related facts wherever possible.
- Practise counting on and back regularly to form the basis of addition and subtraction work (particularly using number lines) and to assist children in learning multiples for multiplication and division calculations.
- When asking oral calculation questions use a wide range of vocabulary so that pupils become secure in their meaning.
- When using and teaching mental calculation strategies ensure that children are given every opportunity to describe methods for themselves and to explain their reasoning. Discuss common errors and those that arise so that pupils can learn from these.
- Ensure that decimal work forms a significant part of mental work to encourage children to become confident in dealing with both whole numbers and decimals in a range of situations and understand the links between the two.
- Encourage children to observe and describe patterns whenever they see them, such as noticing that 4 × 9 is related to 4 × 90 or 0.4 × 9. Use grids, such as those shown below, to draw attention to such patterns.

Teaching resources

ITP number line software, bead strings, pegs on a line, spreadsheets, number lines, digit cards, counting equipment.

Beadstrings for dividing 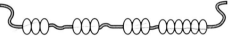 *and arrays*

Number lines, such as those shown below can be used for demonstrating different methods for solving the same problem, e.g. finding a difference by counting on from the smaller to the larger number or counting back from the larger to the smaller.

$7.4 - 2.7 =$

+0.3   +4   +0.4

2.7 3   7   7.4

$7.4 - 2.7 =$

−0.3 −0.4   −2

4.7 5.0 5.4   7.4

Grids such as those shown here.

+	3	9	5	7
8				
58				

×	3	8	9	6
5				
0.5				
0.05				

Counting sticks and number lines – count on in 10s, 100s, 1000s from any number for place value work, in any sized steps beyond zero for negative number work, in fractional steps and using measurement (including temperature).

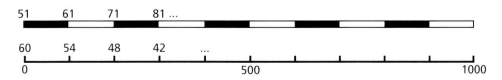

51   61   71   81 …

60   54   48   42   …

0   500   1000

Review and access prior learning
Errors and misconceptions – System scan 1

PART A

1 Observe which words children are familiar with and make a note of those terms, such as product or difference, that children fail to address correctly. Also note whether children work less confidently with decimals as this may suggest a need for greater focus on these (e.g. moving on to Unit 2F rather than others suggested).

2 Encourage children to explain how they worked out each answer. Observe whether they understand the relationships between numbers that are 10, 100 or 1000 times smaller or larger and whether they understand how multiplication and division are related. Unit 2D may be most appropriate for children who do not appear to appreciate the nature of making a question 10, 100 or 1000 times smaller or larger.

3 Observe whether the child makes a connection between tables facts and these questions, e.g. 9 × 4 and 90 × 4. Ask the child to explain what the ° symbol is and note whether knowledge of angle is used in answering the questions.

4 Note whether the child attempts to use a written method or whether he or she rounds and works mentally as is most appropriate. Further rounding questions could be asked to identify whether any difficulties may be caused by rounding or whether errors result from calculation mistakes.

PART B

1 Allow children to use a number line or to make their own notes when answering these questions. Does the child appear to understand the nature
of decimals and the value of the digits? If not, they should be directed towards Units 2E and then 2F that specifically address the nature of decimals and how to calculate with them.

2 Does the child use their knowledge of times-tables facts? It may be appropriate to ask further tables questions to determine whether these are known and to see whether the child can make the link between them and these decimal questions.

3 Observe children's confidence in dealing with calculations through using number lines. Also ask them to make notes or draw their own number lines for a variety of other calculation questions such as those in question 4.

4 How quickly and confidently does the child work with mental addition and subtraction? Using other questions on these two pages, attempt to build a picture of how well the child calculates mentally. Are tables known and secure? How well are addition and subtraction facts drawn upon and used? What other strategies does the child use to find answers? Are they suitable or ineffective strategies?

5 If the child seems unable to answer these questions, ask him or her to say how many millilitres are the same as one litre. If this is the initial area of difficulty, explain that there are 1000 ml in the container and then encourage them to complete the questions.

Answers to System scans

PART A
1a 48 **b** 79 **c** 66 **d** 5 **e** 2 **f** 93 **g** 12 **h** 1.2 **i** 6.2 **j** 1, 2, 4, 8 **k** 3.6 **l** 1.7 **m** 0.7
2a 350 **b** 3500 **c** 3.5 **d** 0.35 **e** 0.35 **f** 35 000 **g** 50 **h** 0.5
3a 180° **b** 360° **c** 210° **d** 90° **e** 270° **f** 270° **g** 90° **h** 90°
4a £23.96 **b** £23.97 **c** £44.90

PART B
1a 2.51 and 1.5 **b** 0.07 and 1.05 **c** 3.7 and 1.5 **d** 2.89 and 1.5
2a 1.5 **b** 4 **c** 0.6 **d** 0.15 **e** 0.6 **f** 0.9
3a 44 **b** 93 **c** 1 hr 44 minutes
4a 43 **b** 53 **c** 76 **d** 77 **e** 91 **f** 102 **g** 101 **h** 68
5a 500 **b** 250 **c** 750 **d** 100 **e** 200 **f** 400 **g** 700 **h** 800

More information and answers to the Check-up scans (follow-up assessments) can be found under the relevant unit section, e.g. if Unit 2F has been used to address a mental skill from the objective list then turn to the back of Unit 2 in this book to find the appropriate answers.

'I can' statements

• I can use mental calculation strategies for addition, subtraction, multiplication and division.
• I can use mental methods for calculations that involve decimals.
• I can record my working for mental methods that involve several steps.
• I can choose when to use mental methods, when to use written methods and when to use a calculator.

Unit 2 Understanding and using place value

Objectives

PB pages 12–23 Understanding of numbers

Objectives	Lesson
• find the value of each digit in large numbers and decimals • order a set of numbers by identifying significant digits	**Lesson 2A** PB pp 12, 13 *PCM 1*
• position numbers on a number line • round whole numbers to the nearest 10, 100 or 1000	**Lesson 2B** PB pp 14, 15
• round decimal numbers to the nearest whole number • use rounding to find an approximate answer before tackling tricky calculations	**Lesson 3C** PB pp 16, 17
• multiply and divide whole numbers by 10, 100 or 1000 • use a known fact to answer linked decimal facts	**Lesson 2D** PB pp 18, 19 *PCM 2*
• create and continue number sequences involving decimal numbers • interpret decimal numbers in the context of measures such as money and length	**Lesson 2E** PB pp 20, 21
• add and subtract numbers with up to two decimal places • explain their steps in calculation methods referring to the value of digits.	**Lesson 2F** PB pp 22, 23 *PCM 3*

Key vocabulary

digit, place value, number, numeral, position, units/ones, tens, hundreds, thousands, tens of thousands, hundreds of thousands, millions, number lines, multiple, round, multiply, divide, decimal, decimal places, approximate

Teaching resources, ideas and mental starters

ITP software, calculators, follow-me cards, measuring equipment, money ...

Counting sticks and number lines – count on in 10s, 100s, 1000s from any number for place value work, in any sized steps beyond zero for negative number work, in fractional steps and using measurement (including temperature).

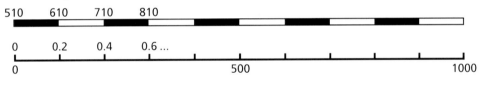

Place value cards, including those for decimals, base 10 apparatus

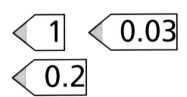

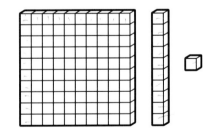

Review and access prior learning

Errors and misconceptions – System scan 2

1. Provide children with place value cards, if necessary, for this question. Observe whether children understand that the position of the digit signifies its value. Do they know the names of the digits to the right of the thousands digit? Are they able to identify the digits to the right of the decimal point correctly?
2. Assist children in reading these numbers aloud. Is the child able to correctly record each number, understanding the positions of the digits? Or does the child write too many zeros, e.g. 400011 for 'four thousand and eleven'?
3. Draw attention to which questions are rounding to the nearest 100 and which are to the nearest 1000. Observe whether a child knows the convention of rounding those ending in 50 or 500 up to the next 100 or 1000, respectively.
4. Observe how well the child rounds decimals and ask further questions about them, e.g. is the decimal closer to 4 or 5?
5. Observe how confident the child is in multiplying or dividing numbers by 10, 100 or 1000. Ask pupils to explain how they worked out each answer, and note whether they appear to understand the movement of the digits, rather than having a misconception of 'adding a nought'.
6. This question explores decimal sequences. Draw attention to the numbers going up in equal steps. Can the child identify the size of the step and find the missing numbers?
7. Allow children to make notes or use any apparatus or diagrams that help them to solve these decimal problems.

Unit 2A – Knowing the value of digits

PB pp 12 & 13

TEACH

Encourage children to warm up, testing their knowledge of numbers ten times larger or smaller in the **Plug in** activity. Ensure that they read the numbers and decimals aloud as part of the **Chat room** activity and draw attention to the fact that decimals can be read in two ways, e.g. 'nought point 7' or 'seven tenths'. Examine the information in the box together, asking pupils to describe what they notice about the digits. Provide place value cards or a place value grid to help children further appreciate the significance of the position of a digit determining its size. Children often make the mistake of believing that the more digits a number has the greater it is, e.g. thinking that 22 959.75 is larger than 24 986.3. Show how the digits should be lined up and compared to help children complete the **Chat room** activity.

PRACTISE

Pupils then can move on to the **Power up** task to practise identifying the value of digits. Provide them with a copy of PCM 1 for questions 2 and 3. If time, children can use the cards for the **Game play** activity, where they say 'Snap' if two numbers have a digit in common. Provide place value cards for support, if necessary.

APPLY

The **Explore** activity requires children to apply their understanding of the value of the digits to give a number that lies between two others. Suggest that children work in pairs to aid discussion.

Unit 2B – Rounding and using number lines

PB pp 14 & 15

TEACH

Work together to complete the **Plug in** activity, reminding children of how to round to the nearest ten. Stress that the answer will always be a multiple of 10 and discuss the convention of rounding up numbers exactly halfway between the multiples of 10, i.e. those ending in 5. Encourage children, in pairs, to work together to identify the positions that the given numbers would go on the number lines in the **Chat room** activity. Help pupils to say which multiple of 100 each number is closer to and to make the link between this task and rounding.

PRACTISE

The **Power up** exercise provides practice in rounding to the nearest 100. Ask children to identify which digit they look at to determine whether to round up or down, e.g. when rounding to the nearest 100 it is the tens digit etc. The second part involves rounding to the nearest 1000. Discuss the similarities in approach, but point out that they will look at the digit to the left (i.e. the hundreds digit) to determine whether to round up or down. Mark answers together and discuss the answers.

The **Game play** activity provides opportunity for practice in rounding numbers and then using them to give an approximate answer to a calculation. Each pair of children will require a calculator for checking to see whose estimate is closer.

APPLY

It is important that children realise how frequently rounding is used in real life, such as when describing quantities and prices. It may be useful to show newspapers or magazines to demonstrate this, e.g. 80 000 fans went to Wembley etc. For the **Explore** activity children should match the descriptions with the items. They could also write their own descriptions involving rounding.

Unit 2C – Rounding decimals and calculating mentally   PB pp 16 & 17

TEACH

Begin by asking some oral questions about numbers that are between 0 and 1. Draw attention to the fact that parts of whole numbers can be described as fractions or as decimals. Remind children that if a whole is split into 10 equal parts each is a tenth and can be written as 1/10 or 0.1. Then ask them to complete the first two rows of the **Plug in** activity and check their answers by counting on in tenths. Next explain that if a whole is split into 100 pieces (or one tenth is split into 10 pieces) each is called a hundredth and is written as 1/100 or 0.01. Ask pupils to complete the second part of the **Plug in** activity and check their answers by counting on in hundredths. Draw attention to which whole numbers decimals lie nearest to and make the link with this and rounding.

PRACTISE

The first **Power up** exercise provides opportunity for children to round decimals in this way. Remind pupils to look at the tenths digit to help decide whether to round up or down. Similarly, the **Game play** activity provides opportunity for children to round amounts of money to the nearest pound. It is important that children realise the importance of rounding decimals when finding approximate answers to calculations. Show how 5.3 can be rounded to 5 and 8.8 can be rounded to 9, making the simple approximation $5 \times 9 = 45$ for the calculation 5.3×8.8. The second **Power up** exercise provides opportunity for children to make approximations in this way. If time, for the **Chat room** activity, pupils can make up further decimal calculations for others to approximate.

APPLY

The **Explore** activity can be used to encourage quick mental calculation by rounding amounts near to a whole pound and then adjusting to find the exact answer, e.g. £5.99 × 4 = £6 × 4 – £0.04 = £23.96.

Unit 2D – Multiplying and dividing by 10, 100 and 1000   PB pp 18 &19

TEACH

Begin by counting on in tens from zero to 100, holding out another finger each time a number is said. Then ask children to answer the questions in the **Plug in** activity. Ask pupils to explain what happens to the digits of a number when it is multiplied by 10. Ensure that children do not see this as 'adding a nought' as this is unhelpful and inaccurate when multiplying decimals.

Similarly, discuss the information in the first **Chat room** activity and encourage pupils to see that there is a movement of the digits, rather than teaching to 'add a nought'. This could be shown practically by moving digit cards across the columns.

PRACTISE

Ask pupils to tackle the first **Power up** exercise using what they have learnt from the information box. The **Game play** activity provides practice in working out how much money is in a bag containing a number of £10 or £100 notes and requires the cards from PCM 2.

Similarly, discuss the second **Chat room** activity and ask pupils to work together to find the answers. Again emphasise the movement of digits, not the removal of a zero or zeros, when dividing by 10, 100 and 1000. Pupils can then tackle the second **Power up** exercise.

APPLY

The **Explore** activity shows how multiplying or dividing by 10, 100 or 1000 can be useful in finding answers to a wide range of calculations that are related to a given one. Demonstrate how to decide whether the answer will be 10, 100 or 1000 times larger or smaller than the given fact and then to multiply or divide the given answer accordingly.

Unit 2E – Understanding decimal sequences

PB pp 20 & 21

TEACH

Begin by revising counting on and back in tenths and hundredths from any numbers before asking the pupils to complete the **Plug in** activity. Check their answers by counting on as a class, discussing how to say the numbers aloud, e.g. 'nine point nine two' rather than 'nine point ninety-two' as some children might mistakenly say. Watch out for those that slip to counting in tenths in the final sequence after 10 is reached.

It is important that children realise that, for decimals, it is not necessary to write the digit zero for the right-hand digit, e.g. 8.0 or 7.50, but that these can be written as 8 or 7.5. This can be discussed and explored through the **Chat room** activity. Explain to children, however, that it is sometimes useful to write the zero when comparing decimals or making decimal sequences, e.g. it is easier to see that 7.5 is larger than 7.49 when it is written as 7.50. Explain that they can write zeros on the end of decimals without changing their value to make them all have the same number of digits.

PRACTISE

Pupils can practise using and continuing decimal sequences through the **Game play** activity and the **Power up** exercise. Encourage children to work together to read the sequences aloud and ask them to explain their reasoning at all times.

APPLY

The **Explore** activity involves categorising lengths of wood, written as decimals, into groups according to their size. Finally, they are asked to order decimals and here they could be encouraged to write all the decimals so that they have 2 decimal places, e.g. writing 2.3 as 2.30 etc., so that they can more easily order them.

Unit 2F – Calculating with decimals

PB pp 22 & 23

TEACH

Introduce the **Plug in** activity and discuss the terms used, e.g. total, difference etc. Ask children to explain how they would work out each answer, encouraging them to see the link between decimals and whole numbers and to use facts that they already know, e.g. $3 \times 4 = 12$ so 0.3×4 is ten times smaller than 12, i.e. 1.2.

Then consider the decimals in the first **Chat room** activity and ask pupils to find totals of pairs of numbers and to record them. Ask pupils to come to the front and to demonstrate how they added them. Show them that they can be added in similar ways to whole numbers and discuss the most effective strategies, including using formal written methods.

PRACTISE

Children can then practise adding pairs of decimals using these methods in the **Game play** activity, which requires a copy of PCM 3, a dice, 2 counters and 2 coloured pencils per pair.

Then consider the decimals in the second **Chat room** activity and ask pupils to find differences between pairs of numbers and to record them. Again ask pupils to come to the front and to demonstrate their strategies, including using formal written methods.

These can then be practised in the **Power up** exercise. Stress the importance of placing the larger number first and then subtracting the smaller number when finding differences.

APPLY

Read through the initial information in the **Explore** activity and encourage children to work out the missing lengths when the pieces of furniture are placed next to each other without a gap. Remind pupils to give the unit each time (m) and discuss how their answers could also be written in centimetres, if there is time.

Answers

System scans

Unit 2 (PB p6)
1a 30   **b** 30 000   **c** 8000   **d** 7 000 000   **e** 0.2   **f** 0.05
2a 4011   **b** 20 006   **c** 43 030   **d** 1 000 001   **e** 5 306 024
3a 7500   **b** 52 000   **c** 48 900   **d** 49 000   **e** 43 100
f 26 000
4a 4   **b** 1   **c** 47   **d** 13   **e** 35
5a, c and **d**
6a 13.5   **b** 1.7
7a 8   **b** 3.8   **c** 5.79   **d** 2.77   **e** 6.87   **f** 1.18

Pupil's Book questions

Unit 2A (PB pp 12–13)
Plug in: a 10 000, 100 000, 1 000 000, 10 000 000
b 0.3, 0.03, 0.003, 0.0003   **c** 700, 7000, 70 000, 700 000
d 20, 200, 2000, 20 000
Chat room: 5 835 047 is the largest number.
Power up: 1a 600   **b** 70   **c** 2 000 000   **d** 9   **e** 0.3
f 0.05   **g** 800 000   **h** 4000   **i** 3000   **j** 10 000

Unit 2B (PB pp 14–15)
Plug in: a 50   **b** 90   **c** 40   **d** 130   **e** 480   **f** 710
g 140   **h** 660   **i** 210   **j** 9430   **k** 4810   **l** 3860
Power up: 1a 3500   **b** 2900   **c** 7300   **d** 4700   **e** 3800
f 7000   **g** 38 300   **h** 48 600   **i** 39 900   **j** 32 100
2 The tens digit
3a 9000   **b** 4000   **c** 27 000   **d** 35 000   **e** 34 000
f 73 000   **g** 39 000   **h** 49 000   **i** 31 000   **j** 36 000
4 The hundreds digit

Unit 2C (PB pp 16–17)
Plug in: 1a 0.1   **b** 1.5   **c** 2.2   **d** 3.3
2a 7.6   **b** 8.9   **c** 9.4   **d** 10.2
3a 8.85   **b** 8.91   **c** 8.99   **d** 9.05
4a 9.12   **b** 7.03   **c** 7.19   **d** 7.28
Power up (1): a 5   **b** 5   **c** 7   **d** 16   **e** 22   **f** 7   **g** 7
h 12   **i** 9   **j** 126   **k** 44   **l** 35   **m** 375   **n** 50
Explore: 1 £27.96   **2** £26.97   **3** £59.88   **4** £23.91

Unit 2D (PB pp 18–19)
Plug in: a 40   **b** 60   **c** 0   **d** 30   **e** 100   **f** 90   **g** 20
Chat room (1): a 850   **b** 4300   **c** 57 000
Power up (1): a 980   **b** 5600   **c** 12 000   **d** 1430
e 20 900   **f** 71 000   **g** 5   **h** 90   **i** 800
Chat room (2): a 720   **b** 21   **c** 83
Power up (2): a 98   **b** 56   **c** 12   **d** 140   **e** 20   **f** 70
g 2.1   **h** 0.08   **i** 3.5   **j** 0.01   **k** 0.64   **l** 0.75
Explore: a 420   **b** 4200   **c** 4.2   **d** 0.42   **e** 0.42
f 42 000   **g** 4200   **h** 4.2   **i** 4200   **j** 42   **k** 42   **l** 4.2
m 0.6   **n** 7   **o** 60   **p** 0.07

Unit 2E (PB pp 20–21)
Plug in: 1 0.5 0.6 0.7 0.8 0.9 1 1.1 1.2
2 2.9 3 3.1 3.2 3.3 3.4 3.5 3.6
3 3.79 3.8 3.81 3.82 3.83 3.84 3.85 3.86
4 9.96 9.97 9.98 9.99 10 10.01 10.02 10.03
Power up: a 10   **b** 1.6   **c** 14.5   **d** 9.7   **e** 9   **f** 6
Explore: 2 2.09 m, 2.24 m, 2.28 m, 2.3 m, 2.42 m, 2.7 m, 3 m, 3.2 m

Unit 2F (PB pp 22–23)
Plug in: 1 1.2   **2** 5.2   **3** 1.6   **4** 7.2   **5** 1.2   **6** 3   **7** 0.7
8 0.15
Power up: a 4.6   **b** 1.35   **c** 0.71   **d** 1.82   **e** 6.05
f 4.13   **g** 7.15   **h** 1.39   **i** 4.02   **j** 1.78   **k** 2.32   **l** 1.18
Explore: a 3.04 m   **b** 2.04 m   **c** 1.34 m   **d** 2.16 m
e 2.75 m   **f** 1.39 m   **g** 2.4 m   **h** 1.99 m   **i** 1.75 m

Check-up scans

Unit 2A Knowing the value of digits (p52)
1a 30   **b** 800   **c** 400 000   **d** 20 000   **e** 0.09   **f** 0.4
g 5 000 000   **h** 4000
2a 312 375   **b** 45 064   **c** 20 405   **d** 1 005 809

Train your brain!
80 017, 80 071, 80 107, 80 170, 80 701, 80 710, 81 007, 81 070, 81 700, 87 001, 87 010, 87 100

Unit 2B Rounding and using number lines (p53)
1a 1900   **b** 3400   **c** 46 700
d 30 000   **e** 24 500   **f** 89 600
2a 2000   **b** 3000   **c** 47 000
d 30 000   **e** 25 000   **f** 90 000
4 Answers could vary from those shown:
a 30 × 30 = 900   **b** 700 × 2 = 1400
c 5000 – 1000 = 4000   **d** 6000 ÷ 2 = 3000
e 20 × 50 = 1000   **f** 210 ÷ 3 = 70

Train your brain!
3450, 3549
7500, 8499

Unit 2C Rounding decimals and calculating mentally (p54)
2a 18   **b** 4   **c** 5   **d** 30   **e** 25   **f** 10
3 Answers could vary from those shown:
a 3 × 3 = 9   **b** 7 × 3 = 21   **c** 50 – 12 = 38   **d** 60 ÷ 2 = 30
e 2 × 5 = 10   **f** 21 ÷ 3 = 7

Train your brain!
£8.50, £9.49

Unit 2D Multiplying and dividing by 10, 100 and 1000 (p55)
1 Yes, he is correct
2a 1820   **b** 20 500   **c** 63 000   **d** 6   **e** 80   **f** 300
g 150   **h** 30   **i** 60   **j** 0.41   **k** 0.65   **l** 2.5
3a 560   **b** 5600   **c** 5.6   **d** 0.56   **e** 0.56   **f** 56 000
g 5600   **h** 5.6   **i** 5600   **j** 56   **k** 56   **l** 5.6   **m** 0.8   **n** 7
o 80   **p** 0.07

Unit 2E Understanding decimal sequences (p56)
1a 5.9, 6, 6.1, 6.2, 6.3, 6.4
b 2.67, 2.68, 2.69, 2.7, 2.71, 2.72
c 9.99, 10, 10.01, 10.02, 10.03, 10.04
2a 8.1   **b** 3.7   **c** 12.2   **d** 9.8
3 0.2, 2, 2.09, 2.49, 2.5, 2.9, 3

Train your brain!
2.06

2F Calculating with decimals (p57)
1a 1.4   **b** 3.4   **c** 1.9   **d** 4.2   **e** 1.8   **f** 4   **g** 0.6   **h** 0.35
2a 8   **b** 3.8   **c** 5.79   **d** 2.77   **e** 6.87   **f** 1.18
Train your brain!
a 0.9 and 1.56   **b** 0.9 and 1.56   **c** 6 and 1.01

Unit 3 Calculating with money and time

Objectives

PB pages 24–33 Calculating using money and time

• read and write the same time, using alternative notations, for example, digital, 12- or 24-hour clock • locate required information in a timetable or a calendar	**Lesson 3A** PB pp 24, 25 PCM 4
• convert between units of time, for example, recognise that 140 secs = 2 mins 20 secs	**Lesson 3B** PB pp 26, 27 PCM 5
• add times and find time differences, converting between units of time as necessary • draw time lines to support accurate calculation involving time	**Lesson 3C** PB pp 28, 29 PCM 5
• break money problems into steps and identify each calculation required • record working for each stage of multi-step problems involving money	**Lesson 3D** PB pp 30, 31
• use calculators to solve money problems, recording each calculation that is done • interpret calculator displays in the context of money, recognising, for example, that 4.2 in pounds represents £4.20 or that 10.6666667 would round up to £10.67	**Lesson 3E** PB pp 32, 33

Key vocabulary

timetable, calendar, year, week, month, day, hour, minute, second, difference, calculate, time line, analogue, digital, money, pounds, pence, problem, rounding, …

Teaching resources, ideas and mental starters

Geared clocks, ITP software, calculators, real price lists, real catalogues, follow-me cards, coins, time lines, real timetables, calendars, squared paper, graphs, tables and charts from magazines & the internet, bus/train/school timetables, data from real-life contexts

Counting sticks Count on in minutes across o'clock times, or in 5-, 10-, 15-, 20-, 30- or 45-minute intervals

11:35   11:45   11:55   12:05 …

To help with converting between units of time count in 7s (weeks to days), 60s (minutes to seconds, hours to minutes), 24s (days to hours), 12s (years to months) etc.

0   60   120   …
0   1   2   …

For money calculations count on, crossing whole pound boundaries.

£0.74   £0.84   £0.94   £1.04 …

Time lines can be used to calculate time differences, e.g. between 3:30 and 6:15.

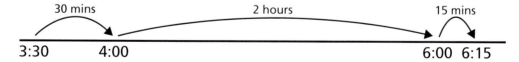

30 mins   2 hours   15 mins

3:30   4:00   6:00 6:15

Review and access prior learning

Errors and misconceptions – System scan 3

1a Provide children with analogue clocks, if necessary, for this question. Observe whether children merely read the digits on digital clocks, e.g. *three thirty-five*, without being able to express them in different ways, e.g. *twenty-five to four*, or show them on an analogue clock-face.

2 Observe how children work with the calendar and ask further questions, e.g. *Which is the last Thursday in August?*

3 Further questions to ask: *Do you know how many days in a week/hours in a day/minutes in an hour/ seconds in a minute?*

4 Allow children to make notes to help them with this question. Observe whether children draw time lines to help them.

5 Does the child choose the correct operation? Which method of subtraction does she/he prefer?

6 Are all amounts keyed into the calculator in pounds or pence (not both)? How does the child interpret the display 10.3?

Unit 3A – Reading/writing times; using timetables/calendars

PB pp 24 & 25

TEACH

For the **Plug in** activity, hand out the loop cards from PCM 4 and revise telling times in analogue and digital times, together with reminding children of the number of hours in a day and minutes in an hour etc. Show a current calendar and discuss the arrangement of it and how it is used. Discuss the number of days in each month of the year, particularly drawing attention to January having 31 days.

PRACTISE

Ask pupils to work in pairs to complete the **Power up** exercise and then go through the answers, inviting children to explain and point to which parts of the calendar they used to answer each question. Look together at the information box from the **Chat room** activity and encourage children to describe equivalent times using 12-hour and 24-hour times. Ensure that children are aware of the way in which am and pm are used.

The **Game play** activity provides an opportunity for children to practise interpreting times in 12-hour and 24-hour notation. Provide each child with lots of small counters to help them move from one answer to the next. All cards should be covered if matching has been done correctly, with the final card, which does not have a matching answer, showing 'quarter to eleven in the evening', that is: 22:45.

APPLY

For the **Explore** task, ask pupils to write questions about the bus timetable given. Point out that 24-hour times are sometimes written without the colon, e.g. 1812 rather than 18:12. Once each child has written several questions (with answers), read them out for a class quiz.

Unit 3B – Converting between units of time

PB pp 26 & 27

TEACH

Work together to complete the **Plug in** activity, discussing how the numbers on the counting sticks can be used to help convert between units of time. Encourage children to use their answers to say:

- how many days in 4 weeks (using the multiples of 7)
- how many minutes in 5 hours (using the multiples of 60)
- how many seconds in 7 minutes (using the multiples of 60)
- how many months in 8 years (using the multiples of 12)
- how many hours in 9 days (using the multiples of 24) and so on.

Write a list of the relationships between units of time for children to refer to, e.g. 1 minute = 60 seconds. Children can then use these strategies to solve the problems in the **Power up** exercise.

Encourage children to describe the times in different ways and to use as few button presses as possible.

PRACTISE

Discuss the use of the counting stick to help find equivalent times and provide each child with a copy of the top half of PCM 5 for the **Game play** activity. Assist children in drawing their own lines to help them work out equivalent times. Remind them that $\frac{1}{2}$ minute = 30 seconds and $\frac{1}{4}$ minute = 15 seconds. If time, children can try the same activity for the cards on the lower half of the sheet.

APPLY

Children can then use these strategies to solve the problems in the **Explore** investigation. Discuss the equivalents 1 year = 12 months = 52 weeks = 365 days and provide a copy of this year's calendar for finding exact ages in years, months and days. Discuss leap years and the implications of these for their exact ages if appropriate. Provide them with calculators to help them multiply and ask children to explain their reasoning as they determine which other children they are younger or older than.

Unit 3C – Adding times and finding time differences   PB pp 28 & 29

TEACH

Begin by orally counting on using times, such as:

- in 5s from 2:45
- in 10s from 11:25
- in 15s from 8:30

- in 10s from 6:20
- in 20s from 4:40
- in 30s from 9:17 etc.

Use a clock-face to support the activity where necessary.

Then ask the children to complete the **Plug in** activity and discuss the answers together.

Write the times 5:35 and 6:20 and ask children to read the times, describing them in different ways, e.g. five thirty-five or twenty-five to six, and to show you them on a geared analogue clock. Explain that the lesson will focus on finding differences between pairs of times. Allow them to count around on the clock face to find the difference between 5:35 and 6:20 (45 minutes). Draw two lines similar to those in the **Chat room** activity to show two ways of finding the difference without looking at a clock face. Encourage discussion and help children to talk about the lines in the **Chat room** activity.

PRACTISE

Children can then use these strategies to solve the problems in the **Power up** exercise.

As children move on to the harder problems, help them to realise that the number lines can include hours and then days. Answers can be given in different ways, e.g. 26 hours or 1 day and 2 hours etc.

For further reinforcement, provide each pair with a copy of PCM 5 and a geared analogue clock for the **Game play** activity. The children should only use the cards from the lower part of the sheet.

APPLY

Children can then use these strategies to solve the problems in the **Explore** investigation. Here times are given in 24-hour notation. Again encourage children to draw time lines to help solve each problem.

Unit 3D – Calculation and money problems   PB pp 30 & 31

TEACH

The **Plug in** activity can be used to encourage quick mental calculation of amounts of money. Show how amounts can be rounded to a whole pound and then adjusted to find the exact answer, e.g. £5.99 × 4 = £6 × 4 – £0.04 = £23.96. Remind pupils that when writing money in pounds/pence notation they should not use the letter p, e.g. £3.05, not £3.05p. Discuss also the importance of not mixing up pounds and pence, e.g. when adding £4 and 50p not getting the answer £54 by mistake!

PRACTISE

Pupils can then practice dealing with prices in pounds and pence by solving the problems in the **Power up** exercise. Encourage them to write number sentences to show how they worked out each problem. Discuss the answers together. Working with a partner they should talk about how to solve the questions in the **Chat room** activity. Ensure that they realise that they should divide to find the price of one and multiply to find the price of many. For further reinforcement, ask them to try the **Game play** activity. Each pair will require a set of counters and paper and pencils.

APPLY

The **Explore** activity can be used to discuss ideas of value for money in real life. Further real-life examples from shops or adverts could also be introduced, e.g. buy-one-get-one-free offers etc.

Unit 3E – Using calculators for money problems

TEACH

The **Plug in** activity encourages children to appreciate the value of each digit for amounts of money.

As a group, discuss the prices of the stamps listed in the **Power up** exercise and ask pupils to say how each price could be written in pounds notation, e.g. £0.41. Remind pupils that, when writing money in pounds/pence notation they should not use the letter p, e.g. £3.05, not £3.05p. Discuss also the importance of not mixing up pounds and pence when calculating, particularly when using a calculator.

PRACTISE

Provide each child with a calculator for solving the problems in the **Power up** exercise. Encourage them to write number sentences to show how they worked out each problem and discuss the answers together, checking where errors may have occurred. Help children to correctly interpret the numbers in the calculator display when working with money, e.g. 330 might mean 330p, £3.30 or £330 depending on the question.

Working with a partner, they should talk about the statements in the **Chat room** activity and say who is right or wrong. Ensure that they realise that the 4.2 means £4.20, not £4.02, and discuss how a calculator can show a recurring decimal that needs rounding, e.g. 0.6666667 should be rounded to 67p.

For further reinforcement and practice of these ideas, ask them to try the **Game play** activity. Each pair will require a calculator and a set of counters.

APPLY

The **Explore** activity provides an opportunity for children to remember to work in either pounds or pence when using a calculator to find totals in real life. Further real-life examples from shopping bills could also be used.

Answers

System scans

Unit 3 (PB p7)

1 17:10 = ten past five pm; twenty-five to four in the afternoon = three thirty-five pm; 16:20 = twenty past four in the afternoon; 09:55 = five to ten in the morning
2 Monday
3a 20 **b** 21 **c** 4, 10 **d** 48 **f** 36 **g** 145
4a 32 minutes **b** 2 hours 29 mins or 149 mins
c 1 hour 45 mins or 105 mins
d 6 hours 41 mins or 401 mins
5a £1.88 **b** £14.83
6 £10.30

Pupil's Book questions

Unit 3A (PB pp 24–25)

Power up: **1a** Sat **b** Sun **c** Fri **d** Wed **e** Thur **f** Wed
2a 26th January **b** 22nd March **c** 13th April
3a Monday 18th March **b** Wednesday 20th March
c Tuesday 23rd April **d** Wednesday 15th May
Game play: 22:45 is the final card that does not have a matching time.

Unit 3B (PB pp 26–27)

Plug in: **1** 0, 7, 14, 21, 28, 35, 42, 49, 56, 63, 70
2 0, 60, 120, 180, 240, 300, 360, 420, 480, 540, 600
3 0, 12, 24, 36, 48, 60, 72, 84, 96, 108, 120
4 0, 24, 48, 72, 96, 120, 144, 168, 192, 216, 240
Power up: **1** 1 min 30 s **2** 1 min 1 s **3** 1 min 10 s
4 2 min **5** 10 min **6** 2 min 32 s **7** 3 min 20 s
8 11 min 11 s

Unit 3C (PB pp 28–29)

Plug in: **a** 3:47, 3:52, 3:57, 4:02, 4:07, 4:12
b 7:23, 7:43, 8:03, 8:23, 8:43, 9:03
c 12:55, 1:10, 1:25, 1:40, 1:55
Power up: **1a** 30 mins **b** 42 mins **c** 2 hrs and 31 mins
d 3 hrs and 35 mins **e** 40 mins
2 7 hrs and 58 mins
3 4 hrs and 1 min, 24 hrs, 17 hrs and 30 mins, 25 hrs and 30 mins
Explore: **a** 2 hrs and 30 mins **b** 1 hr and 55 mins
c 1 hr and 35 mins **d** 3 hrs and 25 mins
e 1 hr and 45 mins **f** 2 hrs and 15 mins

Unit 3D (PB pp 30–31)

Plug in: **a** £5.98 **b** £19.95 **c** £2.80 **d** £2.70 **e** £27
f £3.60 **g** £1.80 **h** £7.96 **i** £12.30 **j** £21.35 **k** £3
l £6.25
Power up: **a** £2.10 **b** £2.50 **c** £3.30 **d** £2.35
e £4.60 **f** £2.10 **g** £5.60 **h** £3.50
Explore: **a** Li by 50p **b** Jo by £1.03 **c** Jo by 1p
d Jo by 15p

Unit 3E (PB pp 32–33)

Plug in: **a** £8 **b** 8p **c** £2 **d** 70p **e** 30p
Power up: **1** £3.30 **2** £4.80
3a £3.96 **b** £11.20 **c** £12.30 **d** £8.67
Explore: **a** £8.90, £11.10 **b** £19.07, 93p
c £12.55, £7.45 **d** £12.85, £7.15

Check-up scans

3A Reading and writing times; using timetables/calendars (p58)

1a Monday **b** Tuesday
2a 28th January **b** 25th March **c** 6th April
3a Saturday 23rd February **b** Sunday 7th April
4a 1515 **b** 0425 **c** 2150
5a 8:40am **b** 7:30pm **c** 10:45pm

Train your brain!

a 2039 **b** 1845 **c** 2213

3B Converting between units of time (p59)

1a 7 **b** 24 **c** 60 **d** 60 **e** 12 **f** 52
2 390
3a 30 **b** 3 hours and 30 mins **c** 205 **d** 220

Train your brain!

a £1.05 **b** £1.58 **c** £2.10

3C Adding times and finding time differences (p60)

1 12:04
2 Seven minutes past eleven
3 2 hours and 25 minutes
4 12:10
5 2 hours and 40 minutes
6 18:07

Train your brain!

07:10 12:40, 13:20 18:50, 05:45 11:15,
00:07 05:37, 15:47 21:17, 10:35 16:05

3D Calculation and money problems (p61)

1a £7.98 **b** £34.95 **c** £2.40 **d** £2.40 **e** £18 **f** £3.20
g £2.10 **h** £8.94 **i** £14.35 **j** £18.30 **k** £6 **l** £7.50
2a £2.55 **b** £1.50 **c** £4.55 **d** £9.40 **e** £5.05
f £2.10 **g** £8.40

Train your brain!

Kate pays 66p less

3E Using calculators for money problems (p62)

1 £1.80
2 £5.40
3 £10.30
4 £106.67
5a £6.60 **b** £6.20 **c** £6.70 **d** £6.70

Train your brain!

a £8.90, £11.10 **b** £19.07, 93p **c** £12.55, £7.45
d £12.85, £7.15

Unit 4 Reading scales

Objectives
Most of these objectives are addressed in each of the lessons in Unit 4.

PB pages 34–41
Reading scales

Objectives	Lesson
• work out the size of each interval, count along the scale to check and label marks • recognise how the value of each interval changes when the start or end label changes	**Lesson 4A** PB pp 34, 35
• read values from scales that are horizontal, vertical or circular as on a clock face • identify points between two marks and estimate their value	**Lesson 4B** PB pp 36, 37 *PCM 6*
• interpret scales on graphs and charts, annotating the scale to support accuracy	See Lesson 5C
• use measuring equipment accurately in the context of length, weight and capacity • use their readings to calculate differences and solve problems involving scales	**Lesson 4C** PB pp 38, 39 *PCM 7*
• use the relationship between units of measure to convert units, where appropriate.	**Lesson 4D** PB pp 40, 41

Key vocabulary
problem, scales, reading, axis, horizontal, vertical, weigh, mass, capacity, length, measures, centimetres, metres, kilograms, grams, litres, millilitres, interval, scale, mark, point, interpret, convert

Teaching resources, ideas and mental starters
Measuring cylinder and scales, ITP software, scales and other weighing equipment, containers and measuring cylinders and jugs, tapes, rulers, metre stick and other measuring equipment, thermometer, protractors.

Counting in equal-sized steps is an important skill underpinning scales on axes. This should be in steps of 2s, 5s, 10s, 25s, 50s, 100s, 200s, 250s, 500s and 1000s for children working at this level.

Counting sticks and number lines can be used to reinforce these ideas further and help children recognise and read scales.

Follow-me/loop cards/domino cards can be made (each showing a scale and a reading that matches the scale on another card) and used in a variety of ways, e.g. they can be given out to a group or an individual or used as a basis for oral questions as a warm up to the lesson.

Review and access prior learning
Errors and misconceptions – System scan 4
1   Ensure children understand that they should identify the value of the points shown with arrows, using the given numbers to help them determine the value of the intervals. Observe whether they realise that the intervals on the second scale are different from those on the first, despite the intervals being the same lengths.
2   Is the child able to estimate unmarked measurements on the rulers appropriately? Observe whether he or she tries to split each interval into parts or annotate the scale.
3   Ask the children to explain how they can work out what each arrow is pointing to. Do they try to find the value of an interval or do they just make a guess as to its size?
4   There are several aspects to this question. First does the child correctly read the scale as 140 g? Second, ask the child to say how many grams are in one kilogram (1000) and note whether this is correctly known. Finally, what does the child do to determine how many lots of 140 g are in 1000 g? Observe whether the child adds up lots of 140 g or whether another strategy is used. If the child asks for a calculator, allow them to use one. Then observe whether 1000 g is divided by 140 g and note how the child interprets the display (7.142857143).
5-6   Note whether the child manages to read the scales correctly and whether they are able to give the readings in grams and also in kilograms.

Unit 4A – Understanding scales and intervals   PB pp 34 & 35

TEACH

Ask children to count on in steps of different sizes together before asking them to complete the **Plug in** activity. Encourage children, in pairs, to discuss the **Chat room** activity and to follow the rules given to try to work out the size of an interval on a scale. Ask them to explain what they have read and then to apply it to another scale that you have drawn on the board. Work through the rules together for this scale and discuss any difficulties children experience.

PRACTISE

Children can then work out the numbers marked with arrows in the **Power up** exercise. Make sure that pupils recognise that the value of each interval changes when the start or end label changes.

The **Game play** activity can provide further opportunity for reading scales, where one player in each pair is 'blue' and the other is 'red'. Ensure that children correctly find the totals of their readings, using appropriate calculation strategies.

APPLY

Pupils will require a range of pieces of measuring equipment per pair for the **Explore** activity and some objects to measure. Encourage children to measure carefully and record answers using appropriate units.

Unit 4B – Reading scales and estimating   PB pp 36 & 37

PCM 6

TEACH

For the **Plug in** activity pupils must find the values, one half and one quarter of the way along the line. Encourage them to describe how the halfway number can be used to help find the number one quarter of the way along but watch out for children who incorrectly may just halve each number. This strategy only works when the first number on the scale is zero.

Further questions about the number three quarters of the way along could also be asked, if there is time.

Encourage children, in pairs, to discuss the **Chat room** activity and suggest estimates for the diameters of the coins in millimetres.

PRACTISE

Children can then estimate lengths of the creatures as part of the first question in the **Power up** exercise. The second question explores scales marked in grams. Provide each pair with a copy of PCM 6, a dice and a blue coloured pencil for the **Game play** activity. This provides a further opportunity to interpret scales.

APPLY

The final **Explore** activity requires children to read a wide range of scales in different orientations and showing a range of units. Remind children to give the unit for each scale.

Unit 4C – Solving measuring problems

PB pp 38 & 39

TEACH

For the **Plug in** activity, ensure that children understand that they should find one fifth of the amount of liquid in each container, rather than the amount the container holds.

Encourage children, in pairs, to discuss the **Chat room** activity and suggest estimates for the diameters of the coins, noticing that the coins are not lined up with the zero mark on the ruler. Ask them to explain how they could work out the diameter. Also note that, unlike in the previous lesson where the rulers were marked in millimetres, the centimetres are numbered here. Thus the diameter of the first coin could be written as 3 cm – 0.8 cm = 2.2 cm etc.

PRACTISE

Ask children to play the game in the **Game play** section in pairs. Provide children with the cards from PCM 7. The problems contained on the cards are quite demanding and some children may require support in solving them. Calculators could be provided for further support as the focus is more on reading the scales and deciding how to solve the problem than on calculating.

The **Power up** exercise again requires use of subtraction strategies to find the amount of oil in each container together with addition strategies in finding total amounts of liquid.

APPLY

In the **Explore** problem-solving activity, pupils are required to use appropriate strategies to find the diameters of a range of UK coins.

Unit 4D – Converting between units

PB pp 40 & 41

TEACH

Discuss the questions in the **Plug in** activity and invite children to explain how to multiply and divide by 10, 100 and 1000. If they have already completed Unit 2D, remind them about it or turn to page 18 of the Pupil's Book to look at the **Chat room** activity. Then ask pupils to answer the questions and go through them together, demonstrating the movement of digits to the left or right.

For the **Chat room** section, ask children to talk to a partner about the relationships between units of measurement and to say what the missing numbers are. Go through them together, revising the equivalents 1 m = 100 cm, 1 kg = 1000 g, 1 l = 1000 ml etc.

PRACTISE

For the **Power up** exercise children are required to read the scales and give answers first in grams and then in kilograms. Observe which children may require further support when dealing with decimals (they might benefit from further work from Unit 2).

The **Game play** task is a matching activity. Provide each pair with different coloured counters or cubes to place on matching scales or readings. Note that each scale has two equivalent readings, one in grams and the other in kilograms.

APPLY

For the **Explore** activity, pupils require some measuring scales. These could be electronic or balance scales, as appropriate. Provide a range of items and ask the children to give readings in grams and then to convert the readings to kilograms.

Answers
System scans

Unit 4 (PB p8)
1a 325 **b** 375 **c** 475 **d** 525 **e** 110 **f** 135 **g** 160
h 185
2a 13 mm **b** 32 mm
3a 275 g **b** 475 g **c** 825 g
4 7
5a 8000 g **b** 1100 g **c** 300 g
6a 8 kg **b** 1.1 kg **c** 3 kg

Pupil's Book questions

Unit 4A (PB pp 34–35)
Plug in: 1a 0, 10, 20, 30, 40, 50, 60, 70, 80, 90, 100
b 150, 160, 1870, 180, 190, 200
2a 200, 220, 240, 260, 280, 300
b 400, 420, 440, 460, 480, 500, 520, 540, 560, 580, 600
Power up: 1a 225 **b** 275 **c** 375 **d** 425
2a 160 **b** 180 **c** 220 **d** 240
3a 100 **b** 400 **c** 700 **d** 950
4a 24 **b** 32 **c** 46 **d** 56
Game play: Blue 410, Red 415; Red is higher by 5

Unit 4B (PB pp 36–37)
Plug in: 1a 10 **b** 190 **c** 1250 **d** 300 **e** 100 **f** 60
2a 5 **b** 185 **c** 1125 **d** 250 **e** 75 **f** 45
Power up: 1a 21 mm **b** 18 mm **c** 33 mm **d** 16 mm
e 27 mm **f** 38 mm
2a 225 g **b** 350 g **c** 725 g **d** 575 g
Explore: a 140 ml **b** 2 kg **c** 500 g **d** 60 km **e** 210 g
f 60 ml **g** 3 kg **h** 36 kg **i** 35 cm

Unit 4C (PB pp 38–39)
Plug in: a 5 ml **b** 6 ml **c** 80 ml **d** 16 ml
Chat room: 50 cents coin = 2.2 cm;
Roman coin = 3.1 cm
Power up: 1a 70 ml **b** 40 ml **c** 140 ml
2a 92 ml **b** 72 ml
Explore: 1 1.8 cm **2** 2 cm **3** 2.6 cm **4** 2.4 cm
5 2.2 cm

Unit 4D (PB pp 40–41)
Plug in: a 4000 **b** 1500 **c** 4 **d** 19 000 **e** 150 **f** 25
g 3.5 **h** 1800 **i** 70 **j** 1.75 **k** 0.5 **l** 0.75
Chat room: 1 m = 100 cm, 1 kg = 1000 g,
1 l = 1000 ml, 1.5 m = 150 cm, 2.2 kg = 2200 g,
1.75 l = 1750 ml, 0.7 m = 70 cm, 0.95 kg = 950 g,
0.05 l = 50 ml
Power up: 1a 900 g, 0.9 kg **b** 150 g, 0.15 kg
c 500 g, 0.5 kg
2a 200 g, 0.2 kg **b** 800 g, 0.8 kg **c** 1100 g, 1.1 kg
d 1400 g, 1.4 kg **e** 2250 g, 2.25 kg **f** 2600 g, 2.6 kg
g 3050 g, 3.05 kg **h** 3450 g, 3.45 kg **i** 3850 g, 3.85 kg

Check-up scans

4A Understanding scales and intervals (p63)
1 140
2a 10 **b** 5 **c** 20 **d** 4 **e** 250 **f** 5

4B Reading scales and estimating (p64)
1a 18 mm **b** 33 mm
2a 350 g **b** 675 g **c** 525 g
3a 30 ml **b** 1200 g **c** 3 kg **d** 900 g **e** 17 kg

4C Solving measuring problems (p65)
1a 6 ml **b** 22 ml **c** 150 ml **d** 80 ml
2a 1.3 cm **b** 2.2 cm **c** 3.2 cm
3a 16 **b** 14
Train your brain!
2500 ml

4D Converting between units (p66)
1a 50 **b** 1800 **c** 4 **d** 59 000 **e** 160 **f** 870 **g** 4.5
h 3800 **i** 80 **j** 37.5 **k** 0.005 **l** 0.8
2a 800 g, 0.8 kg **b** 450 g, 0.45 kg **c** 675 g, 0.675 kg
3a 200 g, 0.2 kg **b** 1100 g, 1.1 kg **c** 2250 g, 2.25 kg
d 3050 g, 3.05 kg **e** 3450 g, 3.45 kg

Unit 5 Interpreting tables and graphs

Objectives

Most of these objectives are addressed in each of the lessons in Unit 5.

PB pages 42–51 Interpreting tables and graphs

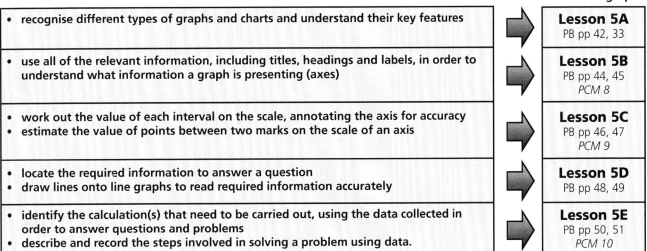

Objective	Lesson
• recognise different types of graphs and charts and understand their key features	**Lesson 5A** PB pp 42, 33
• use all of the relevant information, including titles, headings and labels, in order to understand what information a graph is presenting (axes)	**Lesson 5B** PB pp 44, 45 PCM 8
• work out the value of each interval on the scale, annotating the axis for accuracy • estimate the value of points between two marks on the scale of an axis	**Lesson 5C** PB pp 46, 47 PCM 9
• locate the required information to answer a question • draw lines onto line graphs to read required information accurately	**Lesson 5D** PB pp 48, 49
• identify the calculation(s) that need to be carried out, using the data collected in order to answer questions and problems • describe and record the steps involved in solving a problem using data.	**Lesson 5E** PB pp 50, 51 PCM 10

Key vocabulary

graph, chart, table, frequency table, frequency, bar chart, bar-line chart, pictogram, line graph, pie chart, sector, angle, axis/axes, label, scale, cell, column, row, Venn diagram, Carroll diagram, data, estimate, calculation, problem, multiples, tally, two-way table, interpret, plot

Teaching resources, ideas and mental starters

Data handling and line graph ITP software, square paper, graphs, tables and charts from magazines & the internet, bus/train/school timetables, data from real-life contexts, calendars, travel brochures, sports results, spreadsheets

Use unlabelled Venn and Carroll diagrams and write in numbers to encourage children to guess the criteria you are using. Similarly provide labelled ones and ask children to correctly insert numbers.

Counting sticks and number lines can be used to reinforce these ideas further and help children recognise and read scales, including those presented vertically.

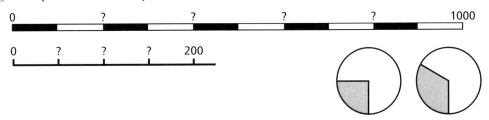

Use two coloured paper (or card) circles each with one radius cut and interconnected to provide practice in identifying and estimating fractions of a whole as the basis for pie chart work, e.g.

Review and access prior learning

Errors and misconceptions – System scan 5

1 Observe how confidently children can give the names of different types of graphs and ask them to explain what features are missing from each, such as a key for the pictogram and pie chart, labels and scales on the bar and line graphs and titles on all of them to show what each is representing.

2 Does the child attempt to understand what the graph is showing? Ask them to explain it in their own words. When interpreting a line graph, note whether the child reads up from the scale to the line and across to the other scale, or vice versa. How accurately is this done? For part c, is the explanation given by the child a reasonable one?

3 When interpreting a pie chart it is vital to know the total number of things (in this case, people) being represented in the graph. Draw attention to this fact and observe whether the child uses this information to see the number represented by each sector of the pie. If so, how is this done? Does the child estimate the fraction of the whole each sector is and then find that fraction of 12? Or does the child work more visually, imagining the pie split into 12 equal slices and counting up how many slices are in each sector?

4 Does the child appreciate the nature of the information being presented in each row and column? Are any errors caused by a lack of understanding of how two-way tables work or are they errors in calculation? Provide a calculator as necessary to focus more on the reading of the table than on calculation skills. Ask further questions of this type to assess this aspect in more detail.

Unit 5A – Recognising graphs and charts

PB pp 42 & 43

TEACH

Ask the children to try the first **Plug in** question and say that you want them to work as quickly as possible. When completed, discuss any strategies used by them and show how the totals of numbers from 1 to 10 can be speeded up using multiplication. Show how 1 and 9, 2 and 8, 3 and 7, 4 and 6 can be paired in tens making $4 \times 10 = 40$, and then adding the final 10 and 5 to give the answer 55. Ask them then to try the second question, grouping pairs with a total of 20 to speed up the process.

Encourage children, in pairs, to discuss the information shown in the **Chat room** section, discussing each chart, drawing attention to the features such as the key, scale, axis labels and titles etc. Spend sufficient time discussing the pictogram, bar chart and table using a range of data vocabulary including the words key, axis, scale, bar, pictogram etc. Encourage children to ask their own questions about the charts, such as those beginning with *How many ... ?* or *How many more ... ?*

PRACTISE

For the first part of the **Power up** exercise children should work with a partner to give 10 true facts about the charts opposite. Assist them in observing a range of different facts, e.g. *the most common sweet colour in a box was yellow, all boxes checked had between 33 and 37 sweets in, the most common number of sweets was 35, more sweets were sold in March than in January*, etc. The second question provides children with the opportunity to see how a pie chart can show the same information as a bar chart but to observe differences: pie charts show proportions more effectively, whereas bar charts make it easier to see the greatest or least values.

For the **Game play** activity, provide children with small blank cards or pieces of paper for them to write questions about the graphs and charts. Tell them to provide answers too. These can then be read aloud to the group as a class quiz.

APPLY

The **Explore** activity provides children with the opportunity to carry out their own survey or investigate other information that could be represented in charts and graphs. This could form the basis of a second lesson or could be completed as a homework activity.

Unit 5B – Interpreting graphs

PB pp 44 & 45

TEACH

The **Plug in** warm-up activity provides children with revision of key calculation vocabulary. Go through the answers and ask children to mark their own work, noting words they misunderstood or calculation errors.

Once completed, ask children, in pairs, to discuss the information shown in the **Chat room** activity, discussing what they think each line graph is showing. Ask pupils to suggest stories that would explain the suspect's movements throughout the day.

PRACTISE

Ask pupils to answer the questions given in the **Power up** exercise, interpreting the data shown in the line graph. Remind them to include a unit in the answer if it is needed. Provide support by demonstrating how to go in a straight line from one axis to the line of the graph and then across or down to the other axis to find answers. Photocopies of the graph can be provided so that children can actually draw lines on the graph itself.

The **Game play** activity provides practice in gathering information from a line graph and pupils in each pair require the cards from PCM 8. Again, the graph could be copied for children to annotate, where necessary.

APPLY

The **Explore** activity can be given as a homework task.

Unit 5C – Estimating points between marks on scales PB pp 46 & 47

TEACH

Ask children to count on and back in 10s, 2s, 5s, 20s, 25s, 50s and so on. Children can then tackle the **Plug in** activity to practise reading numbers on different scales. Note that the red arrows point to marked positions on the scale whereas the blue arrows point to intermediate positions and require estimation. Make sure that pupils recognise that the value of each interval changes when the start or end label changes.

Ask children to look at the line graph in the **Chat room** section and talk to a partner about what they think it shows. Ask them to give an explanation to the rest of the group to explain what the lines represent. Draw attention to the features of the graph, including the scale, the title and the labels on the axes.

Read together the sentences in the speech bubble and demonstrate drawing lines up and across or across and down from one axis to the curve and then to the other axis. Ensure children are confident in doing this.

PRACTISE

In the **Power up** exercise children use what they have been learning about to answer a range of data problems about the line graph, using estimation of the positions on the scales of the axes to find answers. Discuss the answers together and explore reasons for any errors.

Provide children with PCM 9 for the **Game play** activity for further practice in reading scales and interpreting line graphs.

APPLY

Pick one of the cards from PCM 9 and encourage children to tell a story of what might have happened in the filling of the bath etc. Children can then choose their own card for the **Explore** task and write their own graph story.

Unit 5D – Answering questions about graphs PB pp 48 & 49

TEACH

For the Plug in activity, pupils must find fractions of the number 24, as a lead-in to pie charts.

To explore the idea of fractions of a whole circle, ask children to work in pairs for the **Game play** activity. Each child will need a dice and must choose a colour before rolling. For children needing further support in this skill, revise how to estimate fractions by showing a pie split into 12 equal pieces with 1 piece coloured and remind them that this is $\frac{1}{12}$. Colour more sections and explore different ways of giving the fractions, e.g. $\frac{6}{12}$ is the same as $\frac{1}{2}$.

Look at the pie chart in the **Chat room** section and ask children to talk to a partner about what fractions of the pie are the different types of accommodation.

PRACTISE

Children can then tackle the questions in the **Power up** exercise, making decisions about the fractions. For question 3, discuss how, if the pie represent 24 children, then each child's information would be shown in $\frac{1}{24}$ of the pie. If necessary, split the pie into 24 equal sections to help children answer the questions, or alternatively ask them to use their fraction answers to question 2 and find those fractions of 24 mentally.

APPLY

The **Explore** activity shows a bar chart represented horizontally. Children must interpret the information and make decisions about what calculations to use to solve the problems.

Unit 5E – Solving data problems
PB pp 50 & 51

TEACH

The **Plug in** warm-up activity provides children with practice in using known addition and subtraction facts to answer questions mentally. Encourage them to use number lines or notes to help them answer the questions and discuss effective use of diagrams and helpful strategies, e.g. $94 - 29 = 94 - 30 + 1 = 64 + 1 = 65$. Remind pupils to use the inverse operation to check answers. Go through the answers and ask children to mark their own work. Once completed, ask children, in pairs, to discuss the information shown in the table in the **Power up** exercise.

PRACTISE

Children can then answer the questions in the **Power up** exercise, making decisions about what calculations to carry out for each one. Then ask them in pairs to read the question in the **Chat room** section and to talk about how they would answer it. Discuss Carroll and Venn diagrams and encourage pairs to draw either diagram and use it to find the solution to the question. Compare the different diagrams drawn and ask questions about them.

The **Game play** activity provides children with a further opportunity to draw Venn and Carroll diagrams and to use them to sort numbers. They will need a copy of PCM 10, paper, rulers and pencils.

APPLY

The **Explore** activity shows a two-way table. Pupils must interpret the information and solve related problems, using suitable calculation techniques. Remind them to use similar strategies to those used in the **Plug in** activity.

Answers
System scans

Unit 5 (PB p9)
1a From left to right: pictogram, bar chart, line graph, pie chart
b Axis labels/keys and titles missing
2a 15cm   **b** 7:38pm and 7:49pm
c The taps were turned off.
3a 3   **b** 4   **c** 2
4a 44   **b** 75

Pupil's Book questions

Unit 5A (PB pp 42–43)
Plug in: **a** 55   **b** 210
Power up: **3a** bar chart   **b** pie chart   **c** bar chart
d pie chart
4a pictogram and bar chart   **b** pictogram
c two-way table   **d** pie chart

Unit 5B (PB pp 44–45)
Plug in: **1** 28   **2** 99   **3** 75   **4** 4   **5** 4   **6** 82   **7** 1 2 3 6
8 15
Power up: **1** about 10:30am
2 just over 3 hours
3 about 40 minutes
4 at his mother's
5 on the way from his mother's to the station
6 at the bank
7 10km
8 14km

Unit 5C (PB pp 46–47)
Plug in: **1a** 3   **b** 35   **c** 75   **d** 180   **e** 40
2 estimates close to: **a** 0.5   **b** 4   **c** 12   **d** 90   **e** 88
Power up: **1a** 8m   **b** 12m   **c** 0m   **d** $7\frac{1}{2}$m   **e** 13m
2a 10m   **b** 14m   **c** $11\frac{1}{2}$m   **d** 8m   **e** 18m
3a 3 seconds   **b** $2\frac{1}{2}$ seconds
4 1 second and $5\frac{1}{4}$ seconds
5 After 4 seconds
6 $1\frac{1}{2}$ seconds
7 Rob is incorrect. Both throws originated from the height of the children's arms, so would not have been at ground level.

Unit 5D (PB pp 48–49)
Plug in: **1** 12   **2** 6   **3** 8   **4** 2   **5** 4   **6** 3
Power up: **1** apartment
2a $\frac{1}{4}$ **b** $\frac{1}{4}$ **c** $\frac{1}{3}$ **d** $\frac{1}{12}$ **e** $\frac{1}{6}$ **f** $\frac{1}{6}$
3a 6   **b** 6   **c** 8   **d** 2   **e** 4   **f** 4
Explore: **1a** 68   **b** 12   **c** 4   **d** 18
2a 60   **b** 14   **c** 56

Unit 5E (PB pp 50–51)
Plug in: **a** 33   **b** 18   **c** 46   **d** 57   **e** 77   **f** 71   **g** 72
h 65   **i** 91   **j** 57   **k** 62   **l** 55   **m** 59   **n** 91   **o** 78
Power up: **1a** 1   **b** 3   **c** 4   **d** 78
2a 1   **b** 0   **c** 1   **d** 74
3a 1957 and 1967   **b** 1947 and 1957   **c** 1977 and 1987
d 1927 and 1937   **e** 1987 and 1997
4 Satellite channels began
Explore: **1a** 49   **b** 101   **c** 47   **d** 43
2a 80   **b** 80   **c** 80
3 240

Check-up scans

5A Recognising graphs and charts (p67)
1a pictogram or pie chart   **b** any type of table
c line graph or bar chart
2a 64   **b** 67   **c** 15

Train your brain!

true, true

5B Interpreting graphs (p68)
1a 17   **b** 89   **c** 100   **d** 8   **e** 1   **f** 1, 3, 5, 15   **g** 12
2a about 105 beats per minute   **b** 3 minutes   **c** between 5 and 6 minutes   **d** about 72 beats per minute

5C Estimating points between marks on scales (p69)
1a 7, 1.5   **b** 25, 4   **c** 175, 62   **d** 160, 70   **e** 83, 30
2a 42cm   **b** 7:25 and 7:52   **c** The taps were turned off for an interruption, e.g. a phone call   **d** 7:07 and 7:56

5D Answering questions about graphs (p70)
1a 8   **b** 3   **c** 10   **d** 4   **e** 4   **f** 2   **g** 8   **h** 5   **i** 6
2a $\frac{1}{4}$ **b** $\frac{1}{6}$ **c** $\frac{1}{2}$ **d** $\frac{1}{3}$ **e** $\frac{1}{12}$
3a $\frac{1}{4}$ **b** $\frac{1}{3}$ **c** $\frac{1}{6}$
4a 12   **b** 4   **c** 16   **d** 8

5E Solving data problems (p71)
1a 83   **b** 8   **c** 66   **d** 77   **e** 63   **f** 71   **g** 46   **h** 16   **i** 91
j 47
2a 32   **b** 47   **c** 62   **d** 65

Objectives

PB pages 52–63
Understanding of shapes

• describe 2-D shapes using a wide range of properties including number of sides, equal sides, number of right angles, equal angles and number of lines of symmetry	**Lesson 6A** PB pp 52, 53 *PCM 11*
• describe 3-D shapes using number and shape of faces, number of edges and vertices, equal edges	**Lesson 6B** PB pp 54, 55
• recognise parallel and perpendicular lines, including in 2-D shapes • classify a set of shapes using various criteria and record using diagrams including Venn diagrams, Carroll diagrams and tree diagrams	**Lesson 6C** PB pp 56, 57 *PCM 11*
• draw 2-D shapes accurately using different grids or using rulers and protractors	**Lesson 6D** PB pp 58, 59 *PCM 12*
• build 3-D shapes using construction kits or by drawing nets	**Lesson 6E** PB pp 60, 61
• visualise the result of reflecting, rotating or translating a 2-D shape and test their ideas • recognise that the length of each side and the size of each angle do not change when a shape is reflected, rotated or translated.	**Lesson 6F** PB pp 62, 63

Key vocabulary

2-D shapes: circle, rectangle, quadrilateral, rhombus, trapezium, parallelogram, square, triangle, pentagon, hexagon, heptagon, octagon, decagon; 3-D shapes: cone, sphere, cylinder, cube, cuboid, prism, pyramid, sides, edge, face, vertex/vertices (corners), symmetry, right angle, equal, diagonal, regular, rotation, reflection, translation, degrees, angles, convex

Teaching resources, ideas and mental starters

ITP software, pinboards and elastic bands, shape tiles, isometric dotty paper, square dotty paper, squared paper, geostrips, solid shapes, construction kits, hoops for Venn diagram work, interlocking cubes, …

Hide a shape in a cloth bag to encourage good descriptions of the features of shapes. Pupils can ask 20 questions to help them guess the shape.

Visualisation of folding and cutting shapes can test children's understanding of the properties of shapes and their symmetries. Provide descriptions for children to imagine.

Mystery shape: use Venn and Carroll diagrams and suggest which region of the diagram a mystery shape would go in. Encourage children to draw appropriate shapes towards guessing the mystery shape.

Review and access prior learning

Errors and misconceptions – System scan 6

Part A

1a The first question involves identifying numbers of sides, right angles and lines of reflective symmetry of various 2-D shapes. Ask children to give the names of the shapes and to describe any further properties. Look out for whether each child only identifies vertical and horizontal lines of symmetry, e.g. thinking that the equilateral triangle or regular hexagon only have one or two lines of symmetry, respectively.

1b How well does the child interpret what should lie within the rings of a Venn diagram? Is the nature of the overlapping section understood?

2 Provide a set of solid shapes for children to use if they choose for this question. Observe whether the child correctly identifies the appropriate features of the 3-D shapes and whether the words face, vertex (plural vertices) and edge are known and understood.

3 Are the words parallel and perpendicular understood?

4 Provide a protractor and a ruler for this question. Is the protractor correctly used to identify the size of the angle?

5 Note whether the child is able to visualise the folded up net to form a cube.

6 Offer further rotation, reflection and translation questions if the children appear to experience difficulty with this question. Provide them with squared paper and ask them to draw a simple triangle and transform it in given ways.

Unit 6A – Comparing and describing 2-D shapes   PB pp 52 & 53

TEACH

Encourage children to visualise the angles in the **Plug in** activity and to use calculation strategies to work out the sizes of the angles described. Encourage children, in pairs, to discuss the **Chat room** activity and identify similarities and differences between the shapes in each pair. Ask pairs to record their thinking and discuss these together as a group, emphasising correct vocabulary.

PRACTISE

Children can then sample the features of some of the shapes above as part of the **Power up** exercise. Provide each pupil with a large sheet of paper to draw the table and then choose at least three of the shapes to analyse in order to complete the table.

Again, encourage children to work in pairs using the cards from PCM 11 for the **Game play** activity. Discuss the rules of the game and ensure that one child is red and one is blue. Encourage correct use of shape vocabulary and demonstrate how points can be won by identifying in which region of the Venn diagram each selected shape should go.

APPLY

The **Explore** puzzle requires children to draw shapes to match property descriptions. Allow children time to compare their answers and to discuss similarities and differences between them.

Unit 6B – Comparing and describing 3-D shapes   PB pp 54 & 55

TEACH

Ask children to complete the **Plug in** activity, reminding them that there are 1000 ml in one litre. Discuss the answers together and correct any misconceptions.

Give children access to a range of 3-D shapes including a cube, cone, sphere, cylinder, cuboids, prisms and pyramids. Encourage children, in pairs, to discuss the shapes and then to answer the questions in the **Power up** exercise, drawing attention to any vocabulary not known.

Next discuss the statement in the **Chat room** section and ask each pair to explain what they think it means, using some 3-D shapes to check to see if the statement is true, e.g. a cube has 6 faces, 8 vertices and 12 edges, $6 + 8 - 12 = 2$. Note that only 3-D shapes with straight edges and flat faces satisfy the rule, e.g. not cones, cylinders and spheres etc.

PRACTISE

The **Game play** activity can provide a further opportunity for children to analyse 3-D shapes and to identify the number of faces, vertices and edges. Each pair will require a set of 3-D shapes and 2 dice.

APPLY

The **Explore** puzzle requires children to construct 3-D shapes using suitable equipment such as straws, rods or other 3-D construction materials.

Unit 6C – Recognising properties and sorting shapes   PB pp 56 & 57

TEACH

For the **Plug in** activity, ensure that children understand that the perimeter of a shape is the distance all the way around its edge and that a regular shape has sides of equal length. Discuss the use of division for the second question.

Encourage children, in pairs, to talk about the words parallel and perpendicular and determine their meaning in the **Chat room** activity. Discuss them together and ask pupils to say which pairs of lines in the diagram are parallel to each other and which are perpendicular.

PRACTISE

Ask children to play the game in the **Game play** section in pairs. They will need the cards from PCM 11. It is important that they understand how the tree diagram can be used to sort shapes. Before the game, give examples of this together. Explain the rules of the game to them as follows: Children take turns to pick a shape card. They should then, starting at the left of the tree diagram, observe how many sides it has, whether any sides are parallel, and finally whether any are perpendicular. This should lead them to the right-hand side of the diagram where they score a given number of points. They continue in this way until all the cards have been used and the winner is the player with most points.

The activity in the **Power up** section involves the edges of a 3-D shape being parallel or perpendicular. Ask pupils to identify whether each statement is true or false.

APPLY

The **Explore** activity refers to the tree diagram used for the game. It involves explaining why it is impossible to score 50 points in one go, despite two of the right-hand scores being 50. This is because no 3-sided shape can have two parallel sides, so the top two scores can never be reached. Challenge children to draw a triangle with parallel sides to emphasise this point.

Unit 6D – Drawing 2-D shapes   PB pp 58 & 59

TEACH

Encourage children to visualise the angles in the **Plug in** activity and to use calculation strategies to work out the answers. For question 2, remind them that acute angles are more than 0° and less than 90°, a right angle is 90° and an obtuse angle is more than 90° and less than 180°. Children could be asked to sketch each angle for further reinforcement of these terms.

PRACTISE

For the **Power up** exercise, provide children with a copy of PCM 12. Ask them to work in pairs to draw the shapes describe, revising the terms used and encouraging children to say which terms they do not understand. Discuss and compare their answers together.

Encourage children, in pairs, to discuss the **Chat room** instructions for how to draw angles and demonstrate it practically on the board. Help children to draw an angle of their own to your given specification. They can then play the game in the **Game play** section in pairs. Provide children with a ruler and protractor each. After the game, look at some of the angles and lines the children have drawn and ask others to suggest which description in the grid each matches.

APPLY

Provide children with square dotty paper for the **Explore** puzzle. Draw attention to the fact that they should draw a composite shape made from a square and two triangle but only show the outline of the whole shape. They then swap drawings with a partner who must split the shape up into its parts.

Unit 6E – Constructing 3-D shapes   PB pp 60 & 6

TEACH

Ensure children realise that product means multiplying two numbers together for the **Plug in** activity.

Encourage children, in pairs, to work together to discuss the **Chat room** activity, visualising which of the nets fold to make a 3-D cube. Ask them to explain their reasoning.

PRACTISE

The **Power up** exercise requires children to visualise which 3-D shapes will be made from each net. The nets could be photocopied and enlarged to give pupils opportunity to fold and make each of them to check their answers.

For the **Game play** activity, children will need 8 plastic interconnecting equilateral triangles from a construction kit.

APPLY

Discuss the net shown in **Explore** section and ensure that children realise that a dodecahedron is a 12-faced 3-D shape. Provide each child with a plastic regular pentagon to draw around to investigate different arrangements for a correct net. There are a range of possible solutions.

Unit 6F – Transforming shapes   PB pp 62 & 63

TEACH

Discuss the sequences in the **Plug in** activity and invite children to describe in their own words how the shapes in each sequence have been altered (e.g. by rotation through one right angle each time).

For the **Chat room** activity, ask children to talk to a partner about the transformations of the red shape, revising the terms rotation, reflection and translation together. It is important that children realise that when shapes are rotated, reflected or translated the lengths of the sides and the sizes of the angles do not change. Help them to identify which of the shapes is a rotation, which is a reflection and which is a translation of the red shape.

PRACTISE

Provide squared paper for the **Power up** exercise and remind them how to draw a coordinate grid and to plot points. It may be useful to remind them that the first coordinate is how many across from the origin and the second coordinate is how many up from the origin (*Along the corridor and up the stairs*).

Also provide pupils with mirrors and tracing paper to assist them in transforming the shapes. Demonstrate this as a whole group before asking them to try it for themselves.

The **Game play** activity helps children to investigate further transformations and to begin to notice the effect of each transformation on the coordinates of a vertex or point.

APPLY

The **Explore** activity involves identifying which 2-D shapes fit together without leaving gaps. Ask pupils to explain their reasoning and to draw diagrams to show this.

Answers
System scans

Unit 6 (PB pp 10–11)
1a A 4   B 6   C 6   D 3   E 3   F 4   G 10   H 4   I 5   J 4
b A 4   B 0   C 0   D 0   E 1   F 0   G 0   H 0   I 2   J 4
c A 4   B 6   C 2   D 3   E 1   F 1   G 5   H 2   I 0   J 2
2 the yellow rhombus
3a square   **b** 5   **c** 5   **d** 8   **e** all equal length   **f** 2
4a false   **b** true   **c** true   **d** true
Part B
1 The angle is 120° not 60°.   **2** F
3 B yellow, C blue, D orange

Unit 6A (PB pp 52–53)
Plug in: **1** 180°   **2** 270°   **3** 360°   **4** 45°   **5** 30°   **6** 60°

Unit 6B (PB pp 54–55)
Plug in: **1** 500 ml   **2** 250 ml   **3** 750 ml   **4** 100 ml
5 200 ml   **6** 400 ml   **7** 700 ml   **8** 800 ml   **9** about 333 ml
Power up: **1** 3   **2** triangles   **3** 1   **4** 3   **5** rectangles   **6** 1
7 5   **8** 8   **9** cube   **10** true   **11** true   **12** 8

Unit 6C (PB pp 56–57)
Plug in: **1a** 30 cm   **b** 24 cm   **c** 36 cm   **d** 18 cm
e 48 cm   **f** 60 cm
2a 10 cm   **b** 4 cm   **c** 5 cm   **d** 7 cm
Power up: **1** true   **2** false   **3** true   **4** true   **5** true
6 true   **7** true   **8** true   **9** true   **10** true

Unit 6D (PB pp 58–59)
Plug in: **1a** 90°   **b** 180°   **c** 240°   **d** 180°   **e** 270°
f 90°   **g** 45°   **h** 180°   **i** 135°   **j** 180°   **k** 60°   **l** 120°
2a right   **b** acute   **c** acute   **d** obtuse   **e** obtuse
f acute   **g** obtuse

Unit 6E (PB pp 60–61)
Plug in: **a** 12   **b** 9   **c** 20   **d** 15   **e** 30   **f** 18   **g** 24
h 36
Chat room: The following shapes do not fold to make a cube:

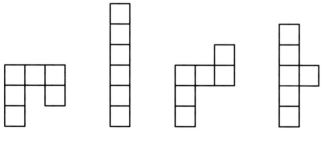

Power up: **1** tetrahedron   **2** triangular prism
3 cylinder   **4** cuboid   **5** square-based pyramid
6 pentagonal-based pyramid   **7** hexagonal prism
8 pentagonal prism   **9** cone

Unit 6F (PB pp 62–63)
Plug in: **1** C   **2** B   **3** D
Explore: The hexagon, square, cross and triangle will fit together without gaps.

Check-up scans

6A Comparing and describing 2-D shapes (p72)
1 6, 2, 2,   5, 1, 2   4, 0, 0
2a the regular pentagon   **b** the isosceles triangle

6B Comparing and describing 3-D shapes (p73)
1a 500 ml   **b** 250 ml   **c** 750 ml   **d** 100 ml   **e** 200 ml
f 400 ml   **g** 900 ml   **h** 600 ml   **i** 333 ml   **j** 667 ml
2a rectangles and triangles   **b** all equal   **c** circle   **d** true
3 6, 8, 12   5, 5, 8   5, 6, 9

6C Recognising properties and sorting shapes (p74)
1a false   **b** true   **c** true   **d** true   **e** true   **f** false
2 All the statements are true.

6D Drawing 2-D shapes (p75)
1a 45°   **b** 360°   **c** 210°   **d** 90°   **e** 270°   **f** 90°   **g** 60°
h 2   **i** 135°   **j** 270°   **k** 45°   **l** 120°
2a right   **b** acute   **c** obtuse   **d** obtuse   **e** obtuse
f acute

6E Constructing 3-D shapes (p76)
1   1, 2, 3, 4, 5, 6
   2, 4, 6, 8, 10, 12
   3, 6, 9, 12, 15, 18
   4, 8, 12, 16, 20, 24
   5, 10, 15, 20, 25, 30
   6, 12, 18, 24, 30, 36
2a triangular prism   **b** cuboid   **c** square-based pyramid
d cylinder   **e** hexagonal prism   **f** pentagonal prism

Train your brain!

The square-based pyramid is the only shape that is not a prism of some type.

6F Transforming shapes (p77)

1a   **1b**

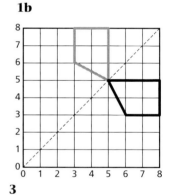

2   **3**

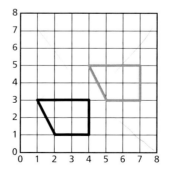
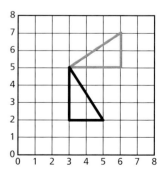

Train your brain!
true

Knowing the value of digits

36 179	5570	249 792
40 101	369 539	16 784
3 652 244	81 273	7 805 021
538 662	29 206	18 015
7 312 400	2 051 431	8227
43 730	9 870 255	2911
2583	8 500 947	178 546
3895	6551	9 454 120
690 882	41 008	28 758
4 217 841	3486	7 777 319

Multiplying and dividing by 10, 100 and 1000

- Each of the bags contains either £10 or £100 notes. The number shows how many notes are in each bag.
- Cut out the cards and put them face down. Each player should pick a card. The player with the most money in their bag keeps the cards.
- The winner is the player with the most cards at the end of the game.

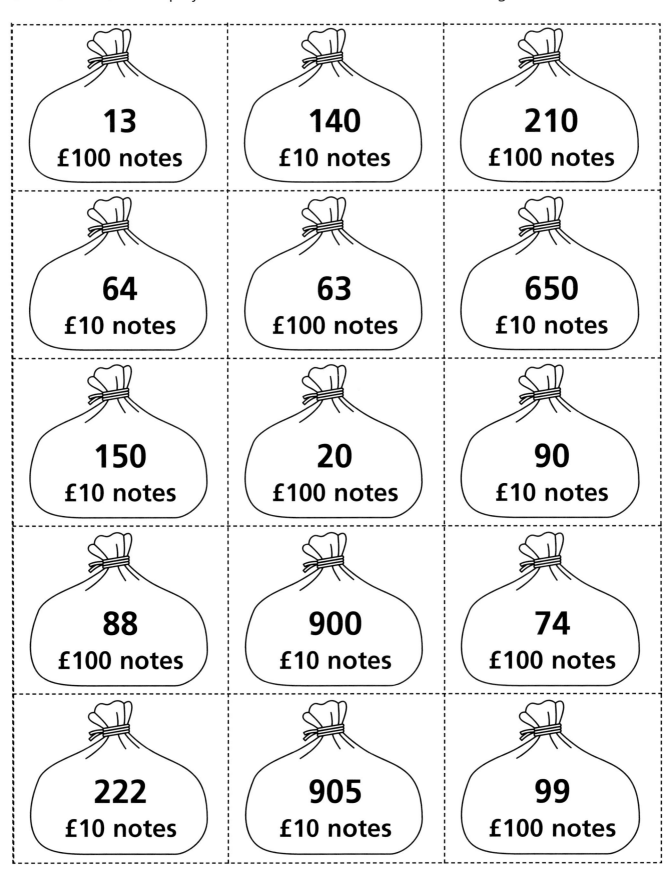

13 £100 notes	140 £10 notes	210 £100 notes
64 £10 notes	63 £100 notes	650 £10 notes
150 £10 notes	20 £100 notes	90 £10 notes
88 £100 notes	900 £10 notes	74 £100 notes
222 £10 notes	905 £10 notes	99 £100 notes

     Shine!/Level 4   PCM 2

Calculating with decimals

2 players

- Take turns to place two counters in different positions on this ring. Roll a dice and move one of the counters on. Find the total of the two numbers.
- If your total is in the grid below, colour it in.

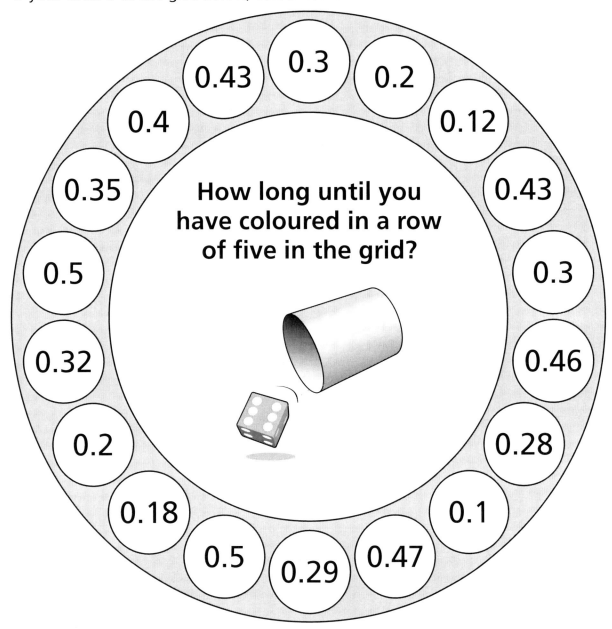

How long until you have coloured in a row of five in the grid?

0.4	0.32	0.22	0.85	0.86	0.93	0.61	0.78
0.9	0.7	0.82	0.79	0.67	0.81	0.56	0.71
0.6	0.97	0.79	0.4	0.39	0.57	0.44	0.55
0.75	0.28	0.6	0.72	0.46	0.13	0.58	0.5
0.68	0.49	0.65	0.4	0.79	0.69	0.62	0.57
0.53	0.76	0.47	0.48	0.97	0.91	0.42	0.62

Reading and writing times

4:15 What is 3:45 in analogue notation?	**Quarter to 4** How many hours are there in a day?	**24** What is 5 to 2 in digital notation?
1:55 What is 10 minutes past 5 in digital notation?	**5:10** How many hours are there in 2 days?	**48** What is 10:05 in analogue notation?
5 past 10 What time is 2 hours after midday?	**2:00pm** What time is quarter of an hour before midday?	**11:45am** What time is 2 hours after midnight?
2:00am What is 4:35 in analogue notation?	**25 to 5** What time is 25 minutes after 5 in the evening?	**5:25pm** What is 10 to 4 in digital notation?
3:50 What is quarter past 9 in digital notation?	**9:15** How many minutes are there in 1 hour?	**60** What is 9:45 in analogue notation?
Quarter to 10 How many minutes are in quarter of an hour?	**15** What time is half an hour before midnight?	**11:30pm** What is quarter past 4 in digital notation?

    Shine!/Level 4   PCM 4

Adding times and finding time differences

0	60	120	180	240	300	360	420	480	540	600 secs
0	1	2	3	4	5	6	7	8	9	10 mins

120 seconds	$2\frac{1}{2}$ minutes	90 seconds	4 minutes
135 seconds	$1\frac{1}{2}$ minutes	30 seconds	5 minutes
300 seconds	9 minutes	210 seconds	$\frac{1}{2}$ minute
360 seconds	$\frac{1}{4}$ minute	150 seconds	6 minutes
570 seconds	$3\frac{1}{2}$ minutes	75 seconds	$2\frac{1}{4}$ minutes
540 seconds	$7\frac{1}{2}$ minutes	195 seconds	$5\frac{1}{2}$ minutes
240 seconds	$9\frac{1}{2}$ minutes	15 seconds	2 minutes
330 seconds	$1\frac{1}{4}$ minutes	450 seconds	$3\frac{1}{4}$ minutes

0	60	120	180	240	300	360	420	480	540	600 mins
0	1	2	3	4	5	6	7	8	9	10 hours

250 minutes	1 hours and 20 minutes
195 minutes	3 hours and 35 minutes
80 minutes	2 hours and 45 minutes
215 minutes	3 hours and 15 minutes
470 minutes	4 hours and 10 minutes
500 minutes	5 hours and 25 minutes
165 minutes	8 hours and 20 minutes
400 minutes	7 hours and 50 minutes
325 minutes	6 hours and 40 minutes

Reading scales and estimating

Play this game with a partner. You will need a dice.
- Take turns to roll the dice.
- Use the key to find how much water must be added to any of your containers. Use a blue pencil to add each new amount of water.
- The winner is the first to exactly fill all their containers.
  (Miss a go if you roll an amount that is more than you need.)

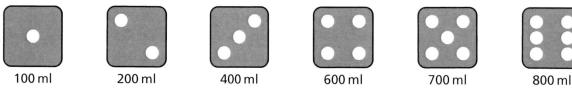

| 100 ml | 200 ml | 400 ml | 600 ml | 700 ml | 800 ml |

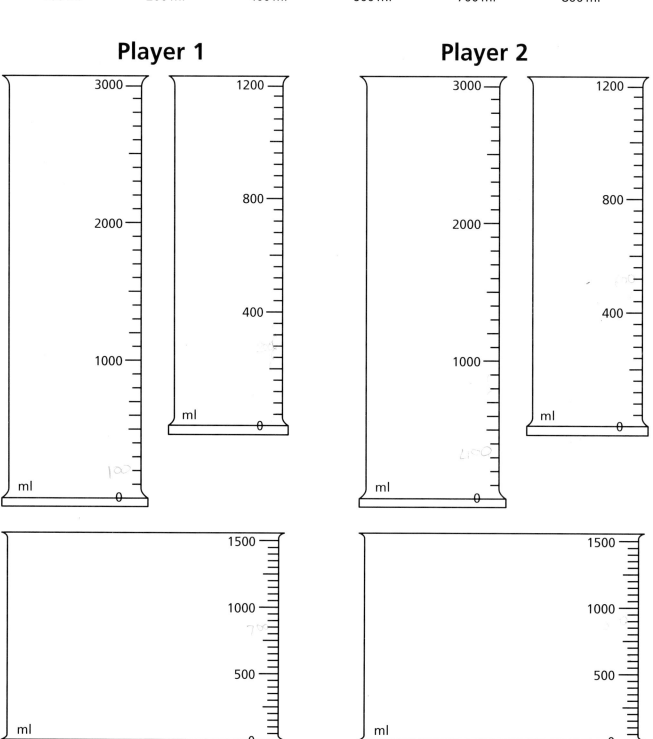

Player 1

Player 2

© Rising Stars Ltd. 2010

Solving measurement problems

One apple weighs this much.

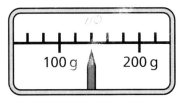

Approximately how many apples will you get in a 1 kg bag?

One pear weighs this much.

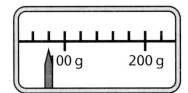

I buy just less than half a kilogram of pears. About how many pears is this?

A baking potato weighs this much.

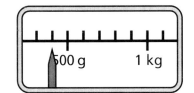

Approximately how many of them would you get in a 5 kg bag?

A coin measures this much.

How many coins would be in a line 220 cm long?

A lawn mower uses this much petrol in one hour.

How much petrol would it use in 5 hours?

A tile is this long.

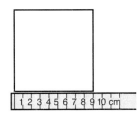

How many tiles would be needed to make a line 54 cm long?

One book is this thick.

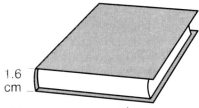

How many centimetres tall would a pile of 5 of these books be?

A CD is this thick.

0.2 cm

How many centimetres tall would a stack of 20 of these CDs be?

A nectarine weighs this much.

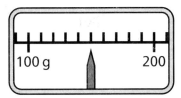

Approximately how many of them would you get in a 3 kg bag?

A shelf is this long.

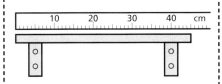

How many books that are 5 cm wide could fit on the shelf?

A banana weighs this much.

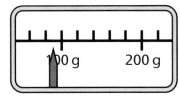

I buy just under $\frac{3}{4}$ kg of bananas. About how many do I buy?

A can of orange holds this much.

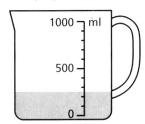

How many cans do I need to fill a 4 litre jug?

Interpreting graphs

What was the footballer's heart/pulse rate at the start of the exercise?	How many minutes from the start of the exercise was the footballer's heart rate first over 100 beats per minute?	What was the footballer's approximate heart/pulse rate after 5 minutes?
What was the footballer's heart/pulse rate after 9 minutes?	How many minutes from the start of the exercise was the footballer's heart rate at its highest?	By how much did his heart/pulse rate rise between the 5th and 6th minute of the exercise?
What was the footballer's heart/pulse rate after 3 minutes?	What do you think happened after 3 minutes from the start and again after 7 minutes?	By how much did his heart/pulse rate drop between the 9th and 10th minutes of the exercise?
How many minutes from the start of the exercise was the footballer's heart rate exactly 60 beats per minute?	When was the footballer's heart rate increasing most?	What was the footballer's approximate heart/pulse rate after 2 minutes?

Estimating points between marks on scales

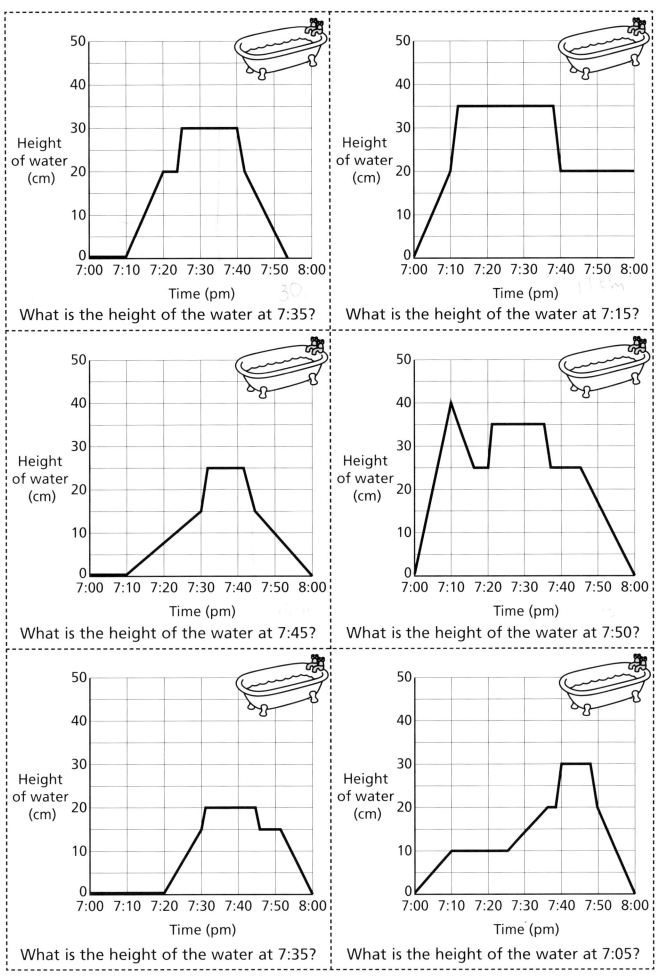

What is the height of the water at 7:35?

What is the height of the water at 7:15?

What is the height of the water at 7:45?

What is the height of the water at 7:50?

What is the height of the water at 7:35?

What is the height of the water at 7:05?

Solving data problems

Work with a partner.
Choose who will be player 1 and who will be player 2.
Follow the instructions for each round and compare your diagrams.

Round 1

Player 1

Draw a Venn diagram labelled:

Even numbers   Numbers less than 20

Put in these numbers:
48	39	38	17	9	14
31	15	12	6	91	30

Player 2

Draw a Carroll diagram labelled:

Even numbers   Odd numbers
Less than 20   20 or greater

Put in these numbers:
48	39	38	17	9	14
31	15	12	6	91	30

Round 2

Player 1

Draw a Carroll diagram labelled:

Multiples of 5   Not multiples of 5
Odd numbers   Even numbers

Put in these numbers:
84	42	33	45	60	70
31	15	12	6	91	30

Player 2

Draw a Venn diagram labelled:

Multiples of 5   Odd numbers

Put in these numbers:
84	42	33	45	60	70
31	15	12	6	91	30

Round 3

Player 1

Draw a Venn diagram labelled:

Multiples of 3   Numbers with the digit 2

Put in these numbers:
24	42	33	45	60	20
31	15	12	6	91	30

Player 2

Draw a Carroll diagram labelled:

Multiples of 3   Not multiples of 3
With the digit 2   Without the digit 2

Put in these numbers:
24	42	33	45	60	20
31	15	12	6	91	30

Comparing and describing 2-D shapes

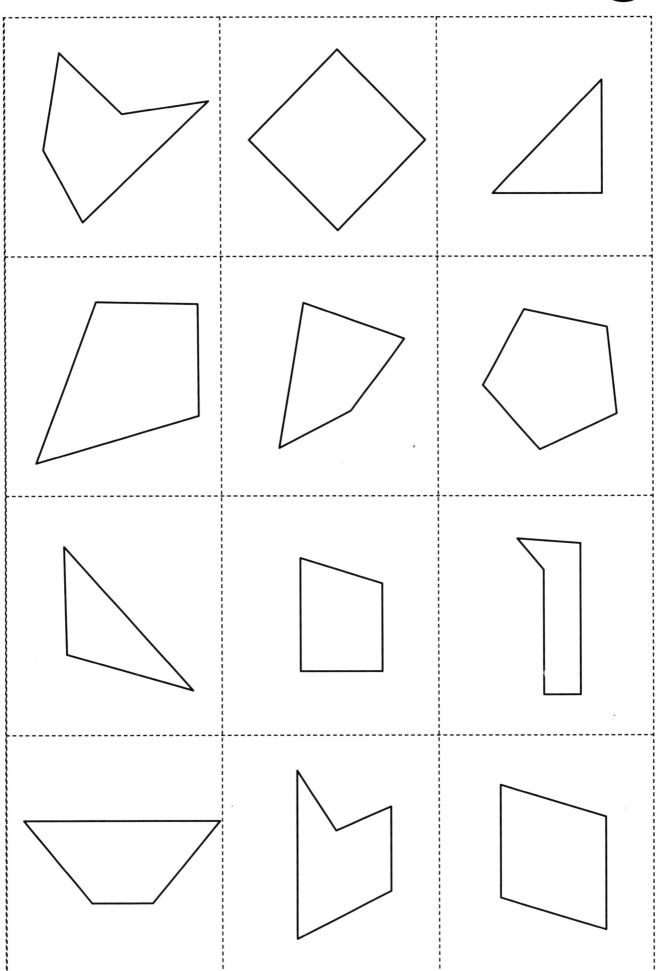

Drawing 2-D shapes

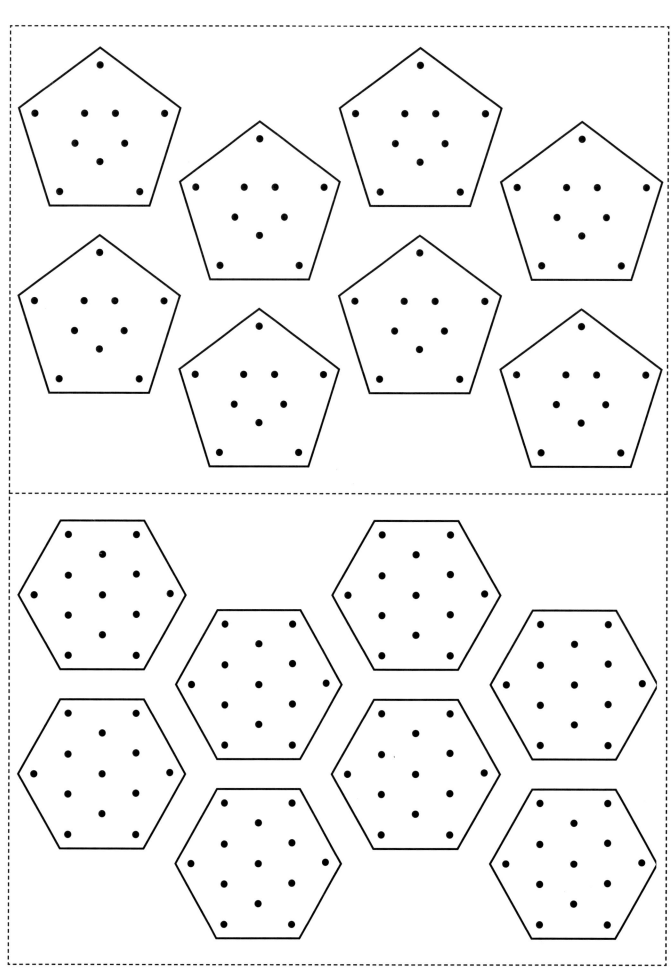

Game play (PB page 20)

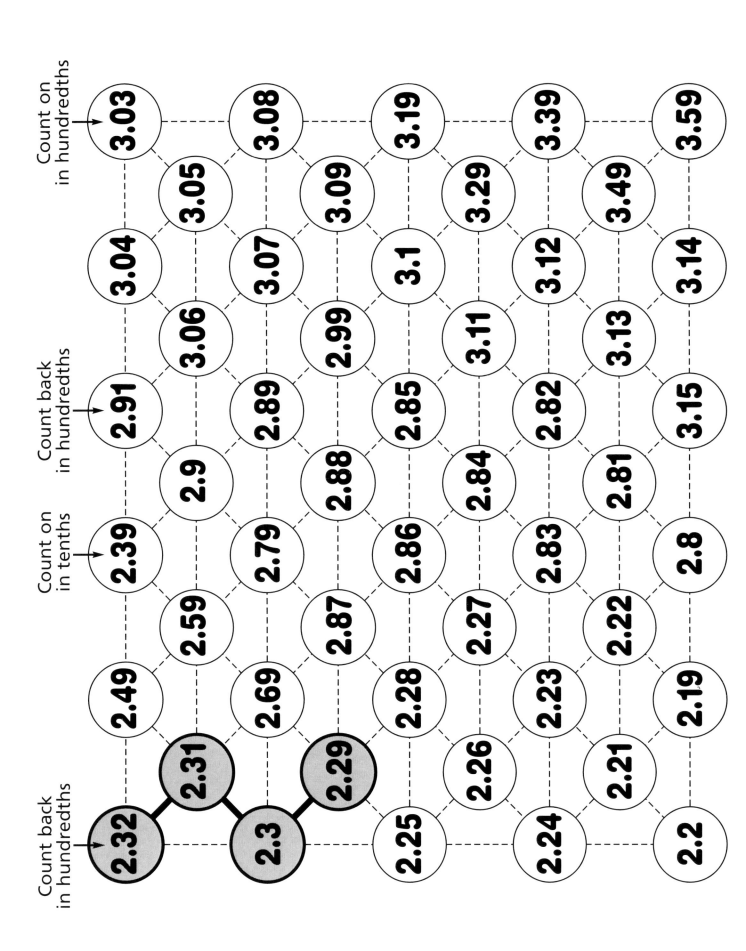

Game play (PB page 25)

You will need: a counter.

- Place a counter on START.
- Find the matching time and move to it, placing a counter on the card you have just left.
- Repeat until all cards have a counter on them.
- Which is the final card that does not have a matching time?
- Write that time in 24-hour clock time.

15:30 Five minutes to nine pm	**03:30** Twenty past six in the evening	**14:05** Quarter to eleven in the evening
17:50 Twenty past seven in the morning	**23:45** Quarter to eleven in the morning	**05:50** Five past two am
10:45 Twenty past seven pm	**20:55** Ten to six in the evening	**05:50** Thirteen minutes past one at night
02:05 Quarter past 12 at lunchtime	**01:13** Five past two pm	**12:15** Quarter to midnight
START Half past three in the afternoon	**19:30** Three thirty am	**07:20** Ten to six am

Game play (PB page 31)

2 players

- Each player starts with £20.
- Take turns to choose items from the grid to buy.
- Work out how much to pay and subtract it from your amount.
- Cover the item with a counter to show it has been sold.
- The winner is the first player to run out of money!

5 eye shadows costing 90p each	12 chocolate bars costing £1.80 for 6 bars	3 magazines costing £1.25 each	12 stickers costing 30p per sticker
12 packets of crisps costing £1.50 for a pack of 4 packets	2kg of grapes costing £3.70 per kg	3 cans of cola costing 45p per can	12 toy cars costing £2.50 for 4 cars
7 pens costing 30p each	12 tomatoes costing 99p per pack of 6	6 chocolate eggs costing 99p for 2 eggs	8 bananas costing 40p each
2 footballs costing £1.95 each	3 packets of sweets costing 75p per packet	8 tennis balls costing £1.99 for a pack of 4 balls	15 pencils costing 40p per pack of 3
8 frisbees costing £1.30 for a pack of 2 frisbees	4 rulers costing £1.25 each	3 CDs costing £1.55 each	7 erasers costing £0.40 each

Game play (PB page 33)

2 players

You will need: a calculator and some counters.
- Each player copies this number line.
- Take turns to pick a question from the grid below and do the calculation.
- Round the answer to the nearest 10p and cross this off your number line, if you can.
- Place a counter on the question in the grid to show it has been used.
- The winner is the player who has crossed off the most numbers on their number line.

£6   £6.10   £6.20   £6.30   £6.40   £6.50   £6.60   £6.70   £6.80   £6.90   £7

£20.17 ÷ 3	£46 ÷ 7	£48.32 ÷ 8	£7 ÷ 3 × 3	£57.86 ÷ 9	£33.54 ÷ 5
£41 ÷ 6	£18.83 ÷ 3	£30.92 ÷ 5	£27.63 ÷ 4	£66.43 ÷ 11	£18.44 ÷ 3
£39.10 ÷ 6	£55 ÷ 9	£51.24 ÷ 8	£6 ÷ 7 × 7	£52.31 ÷ 8	£34.48 ÷ 5
£18.05 ÷ 3	£32.37 ÷ 5	£30.87 ÷ 5	£46.63 ÷ 7	£66.67 ÷ 11	£25.83 ÷ 4
£30.61 ÷ 5	£76.66 ÷ 11	£19.73 ÷ 3	£41.63 ÷ 6	£62.09 ÷ 9	£40.35 ÷ 6
£56.42 ÷ 9	£43.84 ÷ 7	£45.79 ÷ 7	£33.92 ÷ 5	£50.99 ÷ 8	£26.89 ÷ 4

Game play (PB page 35)

2 players: white and black

- Each player finds the value of the arrowed marks in their colour, then works out the total of their readings.
- Which player has the highest total?

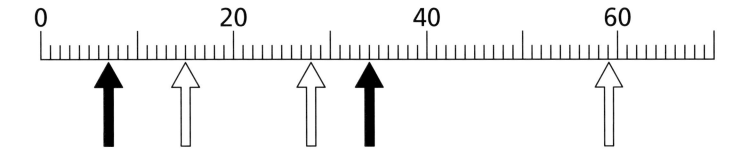

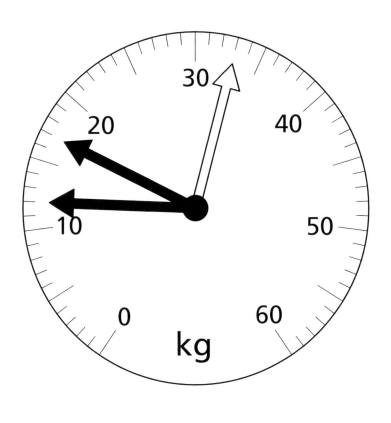

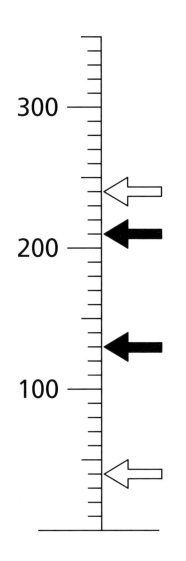

2 players

You will need: coloured cubes or counters.

● Choose a scale and then find the two matching readings.

● Place three counters or cubes in the same colour on them.

● How quickly can you cover all of them?

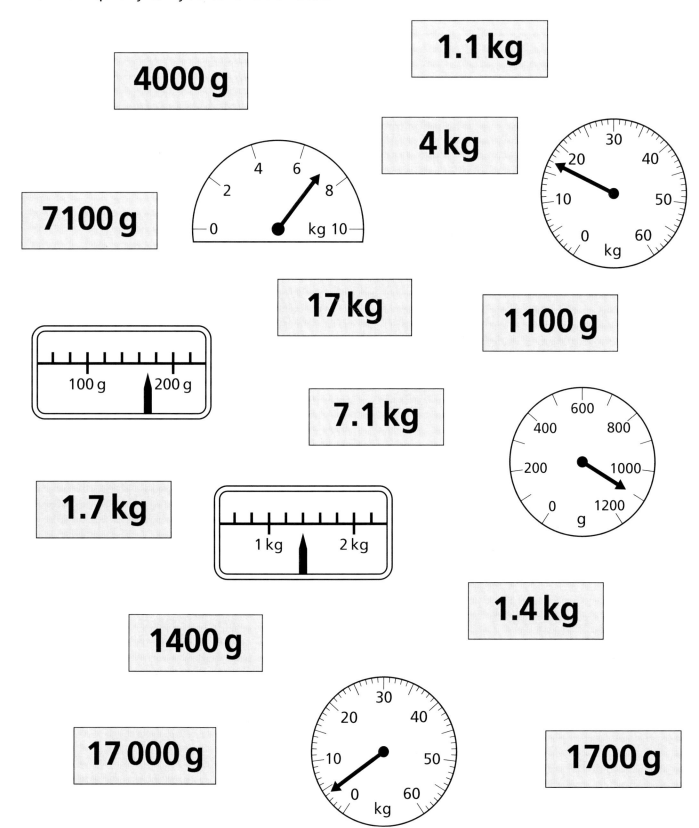

Game play (PB page 55)

2 players

You will need: a set of 3-D shapes and two dice.

- Take turns to pick a shape. Place it on the table below.
- Each player rolls a dice to select 'faces', 'vertices' or 'edges'. Each player counts how many of these the shape has.
- The player with the higher number of faces, edges or vertices scores a point. If you both have the same number, both roll the dice again for the same shape.
- The winner is the first player to score 8 points.

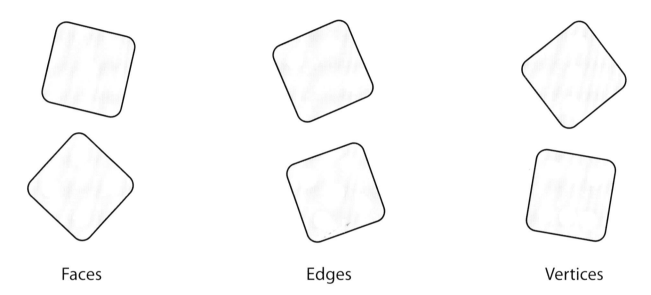

Faces   Edges   Vertices

Check-up scan 2A

Name: _____

1   Write the value of each underlined digit.

a   **63<u>4</u>.6**   b   **5<u>8</u>74.06**

c   **2<u>4</u>38 862**   d   **<u>2</u>2959.75**

e   **0.3<u>9</u>**   f   **472 958.<u>4</u>5**

g   **<u>5</u>835 047**   h   **2<u>4</u>986.3**

2   Write each number in full.

a   300 000 + 10 000 + 2000 + 300 + 70 + 5 = _____

b   40 000 + 5000 + 60 + 4 = _____

c   20 000 + 400 + 5 = _____

d   1 000 000 + 5000 + 800 + 9 = _____

3   Write a number:

a   between 22 000 and 23 000   _____

b   between 900 000 and 950 000   _____

c   between 320 000 and 310 000   _____

Train your brain!

0   7   1   8   0

Write all the possible 5-digit numbers over 80 000 that can be made with these digits.

Now write the numbers in order, starting with the smallest.

I understand what each digit in a large number is worth and can explain how I know.   ☐

Check-up scan 2B

Name: _____

1   Round each of these numbers to the nearest 100.

    a 1853 _____   **b** 3439 _____   **c** 46 695 _____

    d 30 003 _____   **e** 24 505 _____   **f** 89 550 _____

2   Round each of these numbers to the nearest 1000.

    a 1853 _____   **b** 3439 _____   **c** 46 695 _____

    d 30 003 _____   **e** 24 505 _____   **f** 89 550 _____

3   Mark arrows where each of these numbers lie on this line.

1750 4803 6359

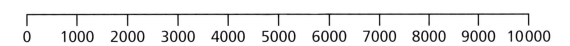

0   1000 2000 3000 4000 5000 6000 7000 8000 9000 10 000

4   Write an approximate answer for each calculation, by rounding each number first.

    a 27 × 31 _____   **b** 689 × 2 _____

    c 4930 − 1151 _____   **d** 5839 ÷ 2 _____

    e 19 × 51 _____   **f** 209 ÷ 3 _____

Train your brain!

What is the smallest number that rounds to 3500 when rounded to the nearest 100? What is the largest number?

What is the smallest number that rounds to 8000 when rounded to the nearest 1000? What is the largest number?

I can round the numbers in a calculation to find an approximate answer. ☐

Check-up scan 2C

Name: _____

1 Mark these decimals on the number lines: **2.8 7.24 4.9 5.3 7.32 7.06**

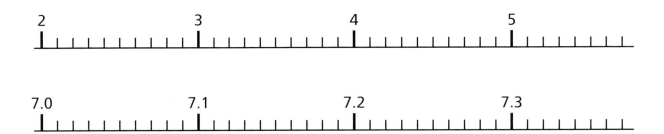

2 Round each of these decimals to the nearest whole number.

    a 18.3 _____

    b 3.9 _____

    c 4.95 _____

    d 30.3 _____

    e 24.5 _____

    f 9.91 _____

3 Write an approximate answer for each calculation, by rounding each number first.

    a 2.7×3.1 _____

    b 6.95×3 _____

    c $49.60 - 11.9$ _____

    d $59.59 \div 2$ _____

    e 1.9×5.1 _____

    f $20.9 \div 3$ _____

4 Give the exact answer to each calculation:

    a £2.99 $\times$ 3 _____

    b £6.95 $\times$ 2 _____

    c £4.98 $\times$ 5 _____

    d £9.90 $\times$ 4 _____

Train your brain!

What is the smallest price that rounds to £9 when rounded to the nearest pound?

What is the largest price?

I understand what each digit in a decimal number is worth and can explain how I know. ☐

I can round the numbers in a calculation to find an approximate answer. ☐

I can use mental methods for calculations that involve decimals. ☐

Check-up scan 2D

Name: _____

1 Sam says the answer to 7.3 × 100 is 730. Is he right?

Explain your answer.

2 Write the answer to each of these.

a   182 × 101

b   205 × 100

c   63 × 1000

d   0.6 × 10

e   0.8 × 100

f   0.3 × 1000

g   1500 ÷ 10

h   3000 ÷ 100

i   60 000 ÷ 1000

j   4.1 ÷ 10

k   65 ÷ 100

l   2500 ÷ 1000

3 Use the fact in the box to help you answer these questions. | 8 × 7 = 56 |

a   8 × 70 =

b   800 × 7 =

c   0.8 × 7 =

d   8 × 0.07 =

e   0.08 × 7 =

f   8000 × 7 =

g   8 × 700 =

h   8 × 0.7 =

i   80 × 70 =

j   0.8 × 70 =

k   800 × 0.07 =

l   80 × 0.07 =

m   5.6 ÷ 7 =

n   5.6 ÷ 0.8 =

o   560 ÷ 7 =

p   0.56 ÷ 8 =

Train your brain!

Use these cards to make as many different true statements as you can, on the back of this sheet.

| 30 000 | 3000 | 300 | 30 | 3 | 0.3 | × 0.3 | × 100 | ÷ 100 |

I can multiply/divide a number by 10/100/1000 and explain how I know the answer.   ☐

I can use number facts to give some linked decimal facts.   ☐

I can use mental methods for calculations that involve decimals and can build on what I know.   ☐

Check-up scan 2E

1 Write the next six numbers in each sequence.

    a 5.6, 5.7, 5.8,   _____ , _____ , _____ , _____ , _____ , _____

    b 2.64, 2.65, 2.66, _____ , _____ , _____ , _____ , _____ , _____

    c 9.96, 9.97, 9.98, _____ , _____ , _____ , _____ , _____ , _____

2 Write the missing number in each sequence.

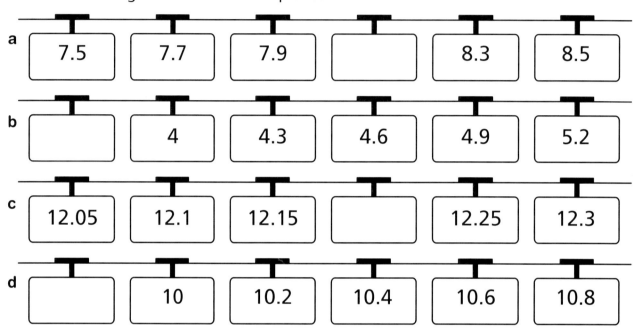

a

| 7.5 | 7.7 | 7.9 | | 8.3 | 8.5 |

b

| | 4 | 4.3 | 4.6 | 4.9 | 5.2 |

c

| 12.05 | 12.1 | 12.15 | | 12.25 | 12.3 |

d

| | 10 | 10.2 | 10.4 | 10.6 | 10.8 |

3 Write these decimals in order, starting with the smallest: **2.5 2.49 2 3 0.2 2.09 2.9**

Train your brain!

Colour the cards showing numbers between 0 and 1 red.
Colour the cards showing numbers between 1 and 2 blue.
Colour the cards showing numbers between 2.5 and 2.7 green.

Which number is not coloured?

2.6	0.5	1.56
2.54	1.88	1.01
1.46	2.06	0.59
0.9	0.75	2.6

I can use mental methods for calculations that involve decimals. ☐

I can find a missing number in a decimal sequence. ☐

I can explain how I order a set of decimal numbers. ☐

Check-up scan 2F

Name: _____

1 Answer these questions.

   a What is the total of 0.5, 0.3 and 0.6? _____

   b What is 1.7 **doubled**? _____

   c What is **half** of 3.8? _____

   d What is the **difference** between 8 and 3.8? _____

   e What is 0.6 **multiplied** by 3? _____

   f How many **lots of** 0.4 are there in 1.6? _____

   g What is 3.6 **divided** by 6? _____

   h What is **half** of 0.7? _____

2 Answer these questions, using a mental or written method.

   a $4.7 + 3.3 =$ _____   **b** $6.7 - 2.9 =$ _____

   c $2.14 + 3.65 =$ _____   **d** $5.98 - 3.21 =$ _____

   e $8.21 - 1.34 =$ _____   **f** $7.03 - 5.85 =$ _____

3 Explain how $6 \times 8 = 48$ is related to the question 6×0.8. Write some more related facts.

Train your brain!

Which pairs of these numbers have:

a a difference of 0.66?

b a total of 2.46?

c a product of 6.06?

3	0.5	1.56
2.54	1.88	1.01
1.46	2.06	0.59
0.9	0.75	6

I can describe each step I do to complete a decimal calculation. ☐

I can choose when to use mental methods and when to use written methods. ☐

I can use mental methods for calculations that involve decimals. ☐

I can use number facts to give some linked decimal facts. ☐

Check-up scan 3A

Name: _____

Look at the parts of a calendar.

1 What **day** of the week is:
   a 25th March?   **b** February 19th?

2 What is the date:
   a exactly one week before February 4th?
   b exactly three weeks after the first Monday in March?
   c of the first Saturday in April?

3 Write the day and date that is:
   a 11 days after 12th February.
   b 16 days after 22nd March.

4 Write these 12-hour times in 24-hour notation.
   a 3:15pm _____
   b 4:25am _____
   c 9:50pm _____

5 Write these 24-hour times in 12-hour notation.
   a 0840 _____
   b 1930 _____
   c 2245 _____

February

S	M	T	W	T	F	S
					1	2
3	4	5	6	7	8	9
10	11	12	13	14	15	16
17	18	19	20	21	22	23
24	25	26	27	28		

March

S	M	T	W	T	F	S
					1	2
3	4	5	6	7	8	9
10	11	12	13	14	15	16
17	18	19	20	21	22	23
24	25	26	27	28	29	30
31						

Train your brain!

Darvel Townhead	1755	1810	1825	1855	1925	2025	2125
West Edith Street	|	|	|	|	|	|	|
Newmilns	1805	1818	1833	1903	1933	2033	2133
Galston Cross	1812	1824	1839	1909	1939	2039	2139
Hurlford Cross	1818	1830	1845	1915	1945	2045	2145
Kilmarnock Bus Stn st 10	1831	1838	1857	1923	1957	2057	2157
Kilmaurs Cross		1841		1907		2007	2107
Stewarton, Avenue Square		1849		1915		2015	2115

Write your answers on the back of this sheet.

a What time is the bus from Galston Cross that would get Jo to Stewarton before 9pm?

b Sam catches the 1825 bus from Darvel Townhead. What time will he arrive at Hurlford Cross?

c The last bus arrives at Newmilns 40 minutes late. What time does it arrive?

I can solve problems that involve time. ☐

I can read a timetable/calendar in order to solve a problem. ☐

Check-up scan 3B

Name: _____

1 Fill in the missing numbers.

   a 1 week = _____ days   **b** 1 day = _____ hours

   c 1 hour = _____ minutes   **d** 1 minute = _____ seconds

   e 1 year = _____ months   **f** 1 year = _____ weeks

2 Use this number line to convert $6\frac{1}{2}$ minutes to seconds.

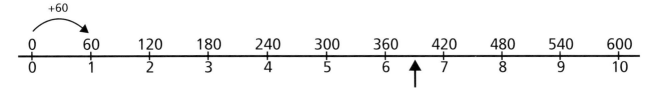

3 Which numbers are missing? Explain your working.

   a 150 secs = 2 mins and ___ secs   **b** 210 mins = ___ hours and ___ mins

   c 3 hours and 25 mins = ___ mins   **d** 3 mins and 40 secs = ___ secs

Train your brain!

A mobile phone company charges 50p for each full minute of call time plus 1p for every extra second.

So, if a call lasts 70 seconds (1 minute 10 seconds)
the charge will be
50p + 10p = 60p.

How much will a call cost if it lasts for:
a 125 seconds?   **b** 188 seconds?   **c** 250 seconds?

I can record my working. ☐

I can solve problems that involve time, recording my calculation methods clearly. ☐

Name: _____

1 Mrs Jones sets a kitchen timer for 37 minutes at 11:27.
   When will the timer go off?   [:   ]

2 What time is 4 hours and 17 minutes later than 6:50am?
   Write your answer in words.

3 An aeroplane takes off at 8:42 and lands at 11:07. Draw a number line to help you
   find how long the flight was.

   [hours and   minutes]

4 A train leaves Kings Cross station at 10:35. It arrives in York 95 minutes later.
   What time does it arrive in York?   [:   ]
   Draw a number line.

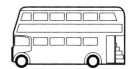

5 A video recorder is set to record from 11:55 until 14:35.
   How long is the recording?   [hours and   minutes]
   Draw a number line.

6 A bus leaves the station every 45 minutes. One bus leaves at 17:22.
   What time does the next bus leave?   [:   ]
   Draw a number line.

Train your brain!

The time in India is $5\frac{1}{2}$ hours ahead of UK time (GMT).

When the time in the UK is [07:10] it is [12:40] India.

Work out which Indian time matches which UK time. Join pairs with a line.

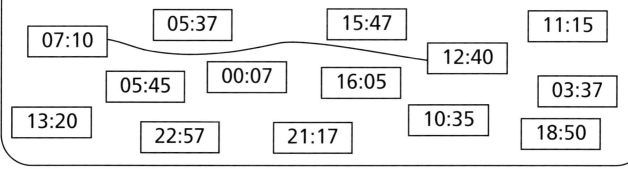

05:37   15:47   11:15

07:10

12:40

05:45   00:07   16:05   03:37

13:20

10:35

22:57   21:17   18:50

I can solve problems that involve time, recording my calculation methods clearly.   ☐

I can add times and find time differences.   ☐

Check-up scan 3D

Name: _____

1 Answer these questions quickly.

a £3.99 × 2 = _____   **b** £6.99 × 5 = _____

c £0.60 × 4 = _____   **d** £0.80 × 3 = _____

e £4.50 × 4 = _____   **f** £1.60 × 2 = _____

g £0.70 × 3 = _____   **h** £2.98 × 3 = _____

i £2.05 × 7 = _____   **j** £3.05 × 6 = _____

k £0.75 × 8 = _____   **l** £1.25 × 6 = _____

2 Here are some greengrocer's prices.

| Peaches 45p each | Brussels sprouts 50p for $\frac{1}{2}$ kg | Cherry tomatoes £1.25 per kg | Grapes £4.70 per kg | Potatoes £2.80 for a 5 kg bag | Cucumbers £0.80 each |

Pineapples £1.20 each

Show your working.

How much does it cost to buy:

a 3 peaches and a pineapple?   **b** 1$\frac{1}{2}$ kg of Brussels sprouts?

c 3 kg of cherry tomatoes and a cucumber?   **d** 2 kg grapes?

e a 5 kg bag of potatoes and 5 peaches?   **f** 2 cucumbers and $\frac{1}{2}$ kg Brussels sprouts?

g 15 kg of potatoes?

Train your brain!

Which girl gets better value for money when buying 8 litres of milk?

Clare buys 8 bottles at 58p per litre.
Kate buys two 4-litre bottles at £1.99 per bottle.

I can solve problems that involve money, recording my working. ☐

I can record my working for mental methods that involve several steps. ☐

I can use mental calculation strategies for addition, subtraction, multiplication and division. ☐

I can use mental methods for calculations that involve decimals. ☐

Name: _____

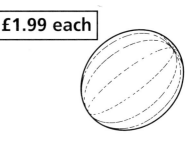

38p each

£2.17 each

£1.99 each

1   Tim used a calculator to work out the price of five bananas at 36p each.
He keyed in 36 × 5 and the display showed 180. How much is this?

2   Ben used a calculator to work out the price of 15 bananas.
He keyed in 15 × 0.36 and the display showed 5.4. How much is this?

3   Jean buys five bananas, a melon and three pineapples.
Use a calculator to find the cost of them all.

4   Simon wanted to share £320 equally between three people. He used a calculator
and keyed in 320 ÷ 3 and the display showed 106.66666667. How much is this?

5   Use a calculator to answer these questions and round each answer to the
nearest 10p.

a   £46 ÷ 7 = _____   **b**   £30.92 ÷ 5 = _____

c   £40.35 ÷ 6 = _____   **d**   £26.89 ÷ 4 = _____

Train your brain!

Use a calculator to find the total of each set of prices and how much change you
would get from £20.

a   45p, £2.55, £1.44, £3.89 and 57p   **b**   89p, £2.74, £7.98, £7.06 and 40p

c   £2.70, £5.39, 43p, £3.94 and 9p   **d**   £4.93, £3.08, £3.66, 38p and 80p

I can use a calculator effectively to solve money problems.

I can choose when to use mental methods, when to use written methods and when
to use a calculator.

Check-up scan 4A

1 The intervals on this scale represent 20. What number is the arrow pointing to?

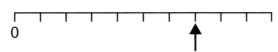

2 Work out the size of an interval on each scale. Explain your method for each one.

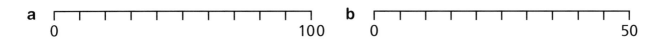

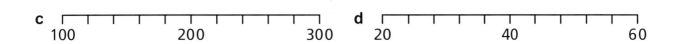

3 For each number below draw an arrow on one of the scales above and label it.

75   220   22   3500   325   2250   390   47

Train your brain!

Write numbers at the start and end of these scales so that each arrow is pointing to the number 160. Make the interval size on each scale different.

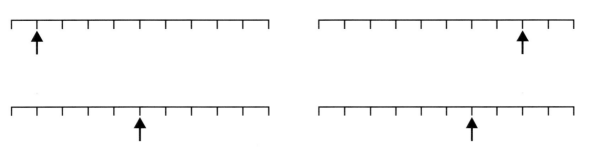

I can work out the size of each interval on a scale and check, using counting. ☐

I can work out the value of any marked point on a scale. ☐

Check-up scan 4B

Name: _____

1 Estimate the length of each creature in millimetres.

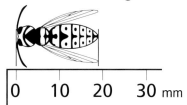

0   10   20   30 mm

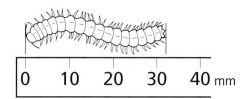

0   10   20   30   40 mm

2 Estimate the mass shown on each scale.

a 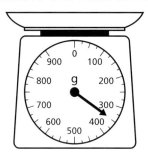   **b** 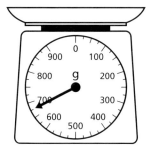   **c**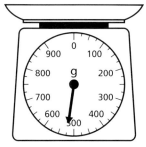

3 Record the reading on each scale.

a
100 ml

0

b
1000 g   2000 g

c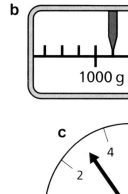

d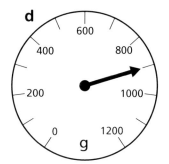

e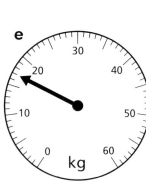

Train your brain!

1200 ml of water is poured into this container.

Use a coloured pencil to show the water level.

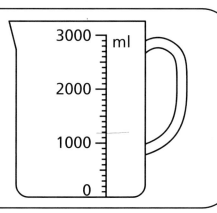

I can work out the size of each interval on a scale and check, using counting. ☐

I can work out the value of any marked point on a scale. ☐

I can estimate the value of a point that falls between two marks on a scale. ☐

Check-up scan 4C

Name: _____

1 Find one quarter of each of these amounts.

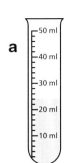 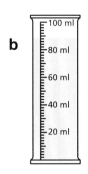 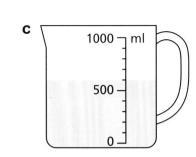 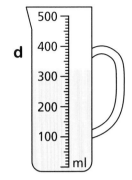

a   **b**   **c**   **d**

2 Use subtraction to find the diameters (the widest distance across) of these coins.

a   **b**   **c**

3 Solve these problems.

    a   A can of orange holds this much.

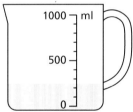

How many cans do I need to fill 4 l jug? _____

    b   An apple weighs this much.

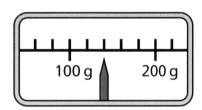

About how many apples will I get in a 2 kg bag? _____

Train your brain!

The following amounts are tipped into this container.
Use a coloured pencil to show the final water level.

1.3 litres   300 ml   0.9 litres

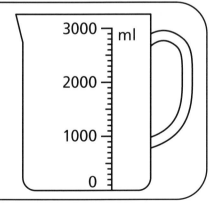

I can read a scale to solve problems involving length, weight and capacity. ☐

I can work out the value of any marked point on a scale. ☐

I can use mental methods for calculations that involve decimals. ☐

Check-up scan 4D

Name: _____

1 Answer these questions quickly.

a 5 × 10 = _____

b 18 × 100 = _____

c 4000 ÷ 1000 = _____

d 59 × 1000 = _____

e 1.6 × 100 = _____

f 8700 ÷ 10 = _____

g 4500 ÷ 1000 = _____

h 3.8 × 1000 = _____

i 0.8 × 100 = _____

j 3750 ÷ 100 = _____

k 5 ÷ 1000 = _____

l 800 ÷ 1000 = _____

2 Read these scales. Write the measurements in grams first, then rewrite them in kilograms.

a 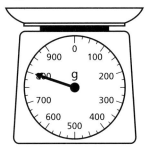 **b** 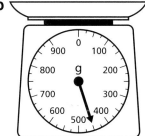 **c**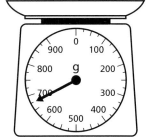

3 Write the mass each arrow is showing in grams, then in kilograms.

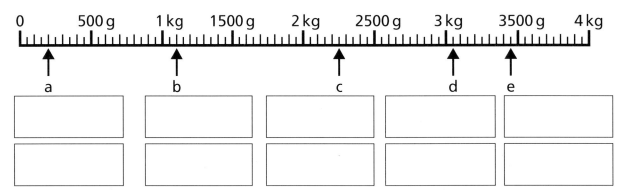

a	b	c	d	e

Train your brain!

Write four masses of your own. Write each in grams, then in kilograms.

I can read a scale to solve problems involving length, weight and capacity. ☐

I can use mental calculation strategies for multiplication and division. ☐

I can use mental methods for calculations that involve decimals. ☐

Check-up scan 5A

Name: _____

1   **a**   What types of tables or graphs need a **key**? Explain your answer.

    b   What types of tables or graphs have **cells**? Explain your answer.

    c   What types of tables or graphs have **axes**? Explain your answer.

2   Look at this table.

A table showing the number of pieces of fruit sold at a school snack bar over a three-week period

	Week 1	Week 2	Week 3
Apples	29	17	18
Pears	30	16	29
Clementines	24	34	44

    a   How many apples were sold over the three-week period? _____

    b   How many pieces of fruit were sold altogether in Week 2? _____

    c   How many more clementines than pears were sold in Week 3? _____

Train your brain!

Some data can be shown in a bar chart or in a pie chart.
Is each of the following statements **true** or **false**?

- *The pie chart is more useful in helping you to see what fraction of the whole each category is.*
- *The bar chart is more useful in helping you to see which category is the largest.*

Explain your answers on the back of this sheet.

I understand the features of different charts and graph.   ☐

I can work out what calculations I need to do to answer questions, using data.   ☐

Check-up scan 5B

Name: _____

1 a What is the **difference** between 46 and 29? _____

b What is the **sum** of 15, 45 and 29? _____

c Find the **product** of 4 and 25. _____

d **Share** 56 equally between 7. _____

e What is the **remainder** when 25 is divided by 3? _____

f Write all the **factors** of 15. _____

g What number under 20 is a **multiple** of 6 and 4? _____

2 This line graph shows a footballer's heart rate during several minutes of exercise.

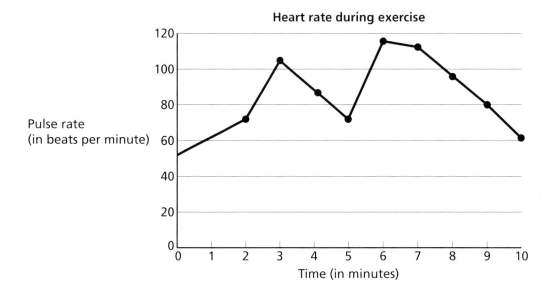

a What was the footballer's heart/pulse rate after 3 minutes?

b How many minutes from the start of the exercise was the footballer's heart rate first over 100 beats per minute?

c When was the footballer's heart rate increasing most?

d What was the footballer's approximate heart/pulse rate after 5 minutes?

Train your brain!

Write three facts about the information shown in the graph above, on the back of ths sheet.

I can use mental calculation strategies for addition, subtraction, multiplication and division. ☐

I can read data accurately from a graph. ☐

Check-up scan 5C

Name: _____

1 Estimate the number each arrow is pointing to.

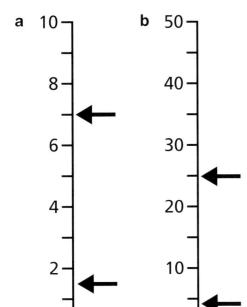

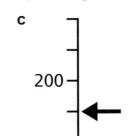

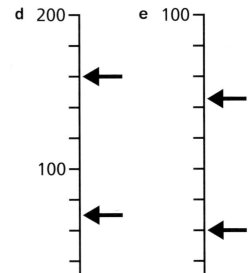

2 This graph shows the water level in a bath between 7pm and 8pm

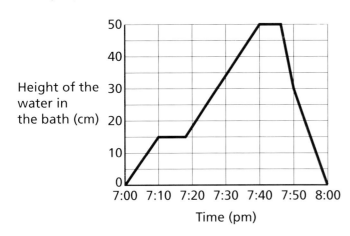

Height of the water in the bath (cm)

Time (pm)

a What was the height of the water at 7:35?

b At approximately what two times was the water level 25 cm?

c What might have happened at 7:10?

d At approximately what two times was the water level 10 cm?

Train your brain!

Write three facts about the information shown in this graph, on the back of this sheet.

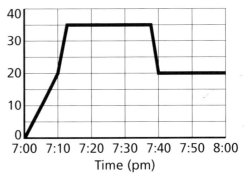

Height of the water in the bath (cm)

Time (pm)

I can find the information in a table or graph to answer a question. ☐

I can read data accurately from a graph. ☐

I can work out what calculations I need to do to answer questions, using data. ☐

Check-up scan 5D

Name: _____

1 Answer these questions quickly.

a One half of 16 =   **b** One quarter of 12 =   **c** One third of 30 =

d One twelfth of 48 =   **e** One sixth of 24 =   **f** One eighth of 16 =

g One fifth of 40 =   **h** One tenth of 50 =   **i** One eighth of 48 =

2 Estimate the fraction of each circle that is indicated by an arrow.

a 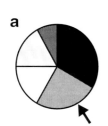   **b** 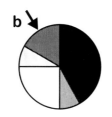   **c** 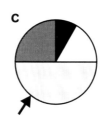   **d** 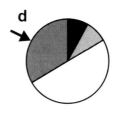   **e**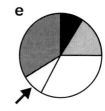

3 48 children have been on holiday.

This pie chart shows where they stayed.

What fraction of the children stayed in:

a a tent or caravan?

b an apartment?

c an hotel?

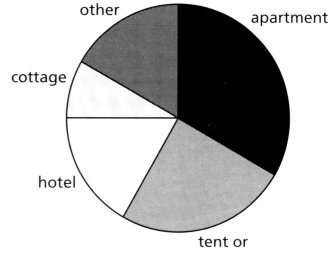

4 How many children stayed in:

a a tent or caravan?

b a cottage?

c an apartment?

d an hotel?

Train your brain!

Write three facts about the information in the pie chart above.

I can work out what calculations I need to do to answer questions, using data.

I can find the information in a table or graph to answer a question.

Shine!/Level 4   Check-up scan 5D

Check-up scan 5E

Draw number lines or make notes to help you answer these questions.

1 **a** 26 + 57   **b** 37 − 29

   c 39 + 27   **d** 49 + 28

   e 92 − 29   **f** 54 + 17

   g 84 − 38   **h** 95 − 79

   i 73 + 18   **j** 75 − 28

2 This two-way table shows some children's favourite type of TV programme.

	Cartoons	Drama/stories	Educational	Quiz shows
Year 4	22	25	6	9
Year 5	16	14	19	16
Year 6	6	40	22	7

How many children:

   a chose quiz shows altogether?   **b** chose educational programmes altogether?

   c from Year 4 took part in the survey?   **d** from Year 5 took part in the survey?

Train your brain!

Write three facts about the information in the two-way table above, on the back of this sheet

I can record my working for mental methods that involve several steps. ☐

I can use mental calculation strategies for addition, subtraction, multiplication and division. ☐

I can find the information in a table or graph to answer a question. ☐

Check-up scan 6A

Name: _____

1 Fill in the table.

Shape	Number of sides	Number of lines of symmetry	Number of right angles
(hexagon)			
(arrow/chevron)			
(parallelogram)			

2 Tick the shape that has been put in the wrong place in each Venn diagram.

a

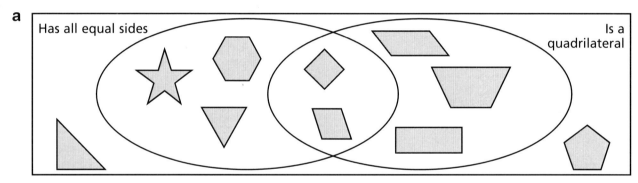

Has all equal sides   Is a quadrilateral

b

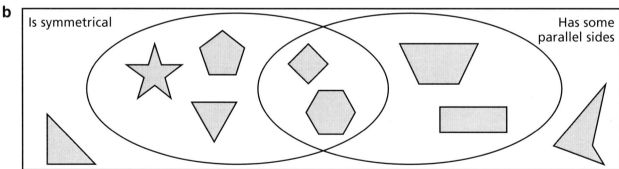

Is symmetrical   Has some parallel sides

Train your brain!

Choose any shape from above.
Write a description of it, on the back of this sheet, so that someone else could work out what shape it is.

I can explain how I have sorted a set of shapes. ☐

I can name shapes and describe their properties, using mathematical language. ☐

Check-up scan 6B

Name: _____

1   A cylinder holds exactly 1 litre. How many millilitres is it holding when it is:

a   half full?   _____

b   a quarter full?   _____

c   three quarters full? _____

d   one tenth full?   _____

e   one fifth full?   _____

f   two fifths full?   _____

g   nine tenths full?   _____

h   three fifths full?   _____

i   about a third full?   _____

j   about two thirds full? _____

2   a   What shapes are the faces of a triangular prism?

   _____ and _____

   b   What is special about the edges of a cube? _____

   c   What shape is the flat face of a cone? _____

   d   A hemisphere is a sphere cut exactly in half. **True** or **false**?

3   Complete the table.

Shape	Number of faces	Number of vertices	Number of edges
cube			
square-based pyramid			
triangular prism			

Train your brain!

Choose any solid shape.
Write a description of it, on the back of this sheet, so that someone else could work out what shape it is.

I can name shapes and describe their properties, using mathematical language. ☐

I can use mental calculation strategies. ☐

Check-up scan 6C

Name: _____

1 Tick to show whether each statement is **true** or **false**.

True? False?

a BG is parallel to AF. ☐ ☐

b AF is perpendicular to FC. ☐ ☐

c FE is parallel to CD. ☐ ☐

d GI is perpendicular to CI. ☐ ☐

e AE is parallel to HI. ☐ ☐

f FC is perpendicular to CI. ☐ ☐

2 Colour the true statements.

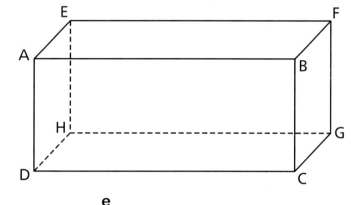

AE is perpendicular to EH.
a

HD is perpendicular to HG.
b

AD is perpendicular to EF.
c

EH is parallel to BC.
d

f
AD is perpendicular to FB.

e
AD is parallel to BC.

g
AB is parallel to HG.

Train your brain!

Draw a pentagon that has both parallel sides and perpendicular sides, on the back of this sheet.

I can name shapes and describe their properties, using mathematical language. ☐

I can recognise parallel and perpendicular sides. ☐

Check-up scan 6D

Name: _____

1 Answer these questions.

   a $180° \div 4 =$ _____

   b $180° \times 2 =$ _____

   c $360° - 150° =$ _____

   d $360° \div 4 =$ _____

   e $90° \times 3 =$ _____

   f $360° - 270° =$ _____

   g $90° - 30° =$ _____

   h $360° \div 180° =$ _____

   i $90° + 45° =$ _____

   j $45° \times 6 =$ _____

   k $90° - 45° =$ _____

   l $30° \times 4 =$ _____

2 Say whether each of these angles is acute, right or obtuse.

   a 90° _____

   b 35° _____

   c 150° _____

   d 100° _____

   e 179° _____

   f 5° _____

3 Use a protractor and a ruler to draw an angle of 68°. Make one of the lines exactly 7 cm long.

Train your brain!

Draw:

a an irregular pentagon.

b an isosceles triangle with an obtuse angle.

I can use mental calculation strategies for addition, subtraction, multiplication and division. ☐

I can draw or make shapes accurately. ☐

Check-up scan 6E

1 Fill in this table to show the different products.

×						
•	1	2		4		
••		4	6			
•••			9		15	
••••		8				24
•••••	5			20		
••••••		12				

2 Name the shape made by each of these nets.

a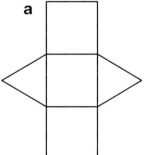

b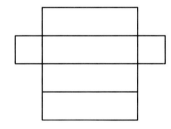

c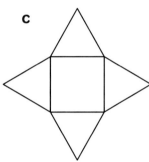

d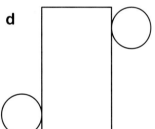

e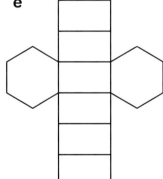

f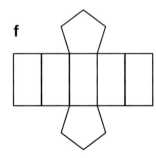

Train your brain!

One of the shapes in question 2 is the odd one out.
Which is it and why?

I can name shapes and describe their properties, using mathematical language. ☐

I can visualise nets of shapes. ☐

Check-up scan 6F

Name: _____

1   Reflect each shape in the dotted mirror line. Write the coordinates of the vertices of each shape and its reflection.

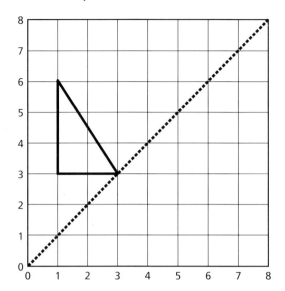   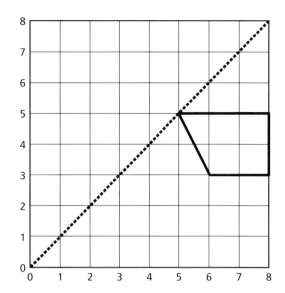

2   Translate this shape 3 places to the right and 2 places up. Write the coordinates of the vertices of the shape and its translation.

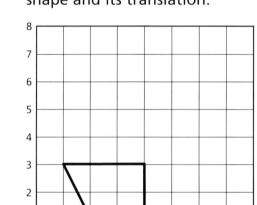

3   Rotate this shape about the point (3, 5) through 90° anticlockwise.

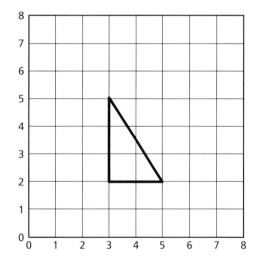

Train your brain!

Is this statement **true** or **false**? Explain your answer on the back of this sheet.

When shapes are rotated, reflected or translated, the lengths of the sides do not change and the sizes of the angles do not change.

I can reflect a shape accurately in a given mirror line.   ☐

I can rotate a shape about a vertex or its centre.   ☐

I can describe where a shape will be after translation.   ☐

Unit 1
Mental mathematics

	😊	😐	🙁
I can use mental calculation strategies for addition, subtraction, multiplication and division			
I can use mental methods for calculations that involve decimals			
I can record my working for mental methods that involve several steps			
I can choose when to use mental methods, when to use written methods and when to use a calculator			

Unit 2
Understanding of numbers

		😊	😐	🙁
2A	I understand what each digit in a large number is worth and can explain how I know			
2B	I can round the numbers in a calculation to find an approximate answer			
2C	I understand what each digit in a large number is worth and can explain how I know			
2C	I can round the numbers in a calculation to find an approximate answer			
2C	I can use mental methods for calculations that involve decimals			
2D	I can multiply/divide a number by 10/100/1000 and explain how I know the answer			
2D	I can use number facts to give some linked decimal facts			
2D	I can use mental methods for calculations that involve decimals and can build on what I know			
2E	I can use mental methods for calculations that involve decimals			
2E	I can find a missing number in a decimal sequence			
2E	I can explain how I order a set of decimal numbers			
2F	I can describe each step I do to complete a decimal calculation or problem			
2F	I can choose when to use mental methods and when to use written methods			
2F	I can use mental methods for calculations that involve decimals			
2F	I can use number facts to give some linked decimal facts			

What I can do in mathematics   Name: _____

Unit 3
Calculating using money and time

	😊	😐	😞
3A I can solve problems that involve time			
3A I can read a timetable/calendar in order to solve a problem			
3B I can record my working			
3B I can solve problems that involve time, recording my calculation methods clearly			
3C I can solve problems that involve time, recording my calculation methods clearly			
3C I can add times and find time differences			
3D I can solve problems that involve money, recording my working for each step			
3D I can record my working for mental methods that involve several steps			
3D I can use mental calculation strategies for addition, subtraction, multiplication and division			
3D I can use mental methods for calculations that involve decimals			
3E I can use a calculator effectively to solve money problems			
3E I can choose when to use mental methods, when to use written methods and when to use a calculator			

© Rising Stars Ltd. 2010

Shine!/Level 4

What I can do in mathematics   Name: _____

Unit 4
Skills in reading scales

	😊	😐	😞
4A I can work out the size of each interval on a scale and check, using counting			
4A I can work out the value of any marked point on a scale			
4B I can work out the size of each interval on a scale and check, using counting			
4B I can work out the value of any marked point on a scale			
4B I can estimate the value of a point that falls between two marks on a scale			
4C I can read a scale to solve problems involving length, weight and capacity			
4C I can work out the value of any marked point on a scale			
4C I can use mental methods for calculations that involve decimals			
4D I can read a scale to solve problems involving length, weight and capacity			
4D I can use mental calculation strategies for multiplication and division			
4D I can use mental methods for calculations that involve decimals			

© Rising Stars Ltd. 2010

Shine!/Level 4

Unit 6
Understanding of shapes

	☺	😐	☹
6A I can explain how I have sorted a set of shapes			
6A I can name shapes and describe their properties, using mathematical language			
6B I can name shapes and describe their properties, using mathematical language			
6B I can use mental calculation strategies			
6C I can name shapes and describe their properties, using mathematical language			
6C I can recognise parallel and perpendicular sides			
6D I can use mental calculation strategies for addition, subtraction, multiplication and division			
6D I can draw or make shapes accurately			
6E I can name shapes and describe their properties, using mathematical language			
6E I can visualise nets of shapes			
6F I can reflect a shape accurately in a given mirror line			
6F I can rotate a shape about a vertex or its centre			
6F I can describe where a shape will be after translation			

Unit 5
Problem solving using tables and graphs

	☺	😐	☹
5A I can understand the features of different charts and graphs			
5A I can work out what calculations I need to do to answer questions using data			
5B I can use mental calculation strategies for addition, subtraction, multiplication and division			
5B I can read data accurately from a graph			
5C I can find the information in a table or graph to answer a question			
5C I can read data accurately from a graph			
5C I can work out what calculations I need to do to answer questions using data			
5D I can work out what calculations I need to do to answer questions using data			
5D I can find the information in a table or graph to answer a question			
5E I can record my working for mental methods that involve several steps			
5E I can use mental calculation strategies for addition, subtraction, multiplication and division			
5E I can find the information in a table or graph to answer a question			